The Insider's Guide to Santorini 2024

By

William F. Peck

Disclaimer

The Insider's Guide to Santorini 2024 strives to provide the most current and accurate information possible at the time of publication. However, the travel industry is constantly evolving, and things can change. We encourage you to double-check opening hours, prices, and other details with the relevant businesses or organizations before your trip.

The authors and publisher cannot be held liable for any errors, omissions, or changes beyond our control that may occur.

While we have included recommendations for various services and activities, these are based on our research and experiences at the time of writing. We do not receive any compensation from the businesses or establishments mentioned in this guide. It is always wise to use your judgment when making choices during your travels.

By using this guide, you acknowledge and accept these terms.

Safe Travels!

About the Author

William F. Peck is a seasoned traveller, accomplished writer, and passionate explorer. As a native of the United States, William has embarked on countless adventures across the globe, from the vibrant cities of Europe to the wild landscapes of Africa, Asia, and the Americas, even venturing into the Polar regions. With a keen interest in cultural immersion and environmental conservation, William has authored several acclaimed travel guides that offer readers an insider's perspective on destinations around the world. His diverse experiences and deep appreciation for different cultures and environments have shaped his approach to travel writing.

In addition to his travels, William advocates for sustainable tourism practices and strives to promote responsible travel behaviours wherever he goes. Through engaging narratives and practical advice, he seeks to inspire others to explore the world with curiosity, respect, and a sense of adventure. When he's not on the road, William enjoys sharing his travel stories and insights through various platforms, connecting with fellow travellers, and fostering a community of like-minded adventurers.

Table of Content

Santorini Travel Guide 2024 by William F. Peck

11

Santorini Itineraries Tailored for Different Travel Styles

Part 1: Planning Your Santorini Escape

Chapter 1: Introduction to Santorini:

Santorini: A Cradle of Beauty Forged by Fire

Santorini, a crown jewel of the Cyclades islands in the Aegean Sea, Greece, isn't just another island getaway. This dramatic landscape whispers tales of a fiery past, boasting a unique beauty sculpted by a colossal volcanic eruption. Steep cliffs plunging into a caldera (volcanic crater) filled with turquoise waters, iconic whitewashed houses adorned with vibrant blue domes – Santorini is a feast for the senses, a place where history and natural wonder intertwine.

A Legacy of Eruption: Santorini's Geological Marvel

Approximately 3,600 years ago, Santorini was a thriving center of Minoan civilization. Then came the cataclysmic event that forever altered its destiny. A volcanic eruption of unimaginable power ripped through the island, blasting away the central portion and leaving behind the now-famous caldera. Ash rained down on Crete, blanketing the Minoan palaces in a shroud of grey, and tsunamis ravaged the surrounding coastlines. This cataclysm is believed by some to be the inspiration for the legendary lost city of Atlantis.

Today, the caldera, a crescent-shaped body of water embraced by dramatic cliffs, is Santorini's defining characteristic. The volcanic activity continues, evidenced by the presence of Nea Kameni and Palea Kameni, volcanic islets within the caldera accessible by boat tours. These islands offer a glimpse into the heart of the volcano, with steaming fumaroles, volcanic rock formations, and even the opportunity to take a mud bath in the sulfur springs.

Beyond the Caldera: Santorini's Diverse Landscape

While the caldera steals the show, Santorini offers more than just dramatic cliff faces. The eastern side of the island boasts gentler slopes covered in vineyards that produce some of Greece's most unique wines. The volcanic soil imparts a distinctive character to the grapes, resulting in crisp whites like Assyrtiko and robust reds like Mavrotragano. Quaint villages nestled amidst the vineyards offer a glimpse into traditional

Greek life. Black, red, and white sand beaches fringe the coastline, each offering a different ambiance for relaxation.

A Journey Through Time: Santorini's Historical Tapestry

Santorini's story goes far beyond the volcanic eruption. Excavations at Akrotiri, a Minoan settlement buried by volcanic ash, have revealed a remarkably well-preserved town with multi-story buildings, frescoes, and intricate pottery. It provides a window into a sophisticated civilization that thrived here millennia ago.

The island's history also reflects the passage of empires. Venetian influence is evident in the architecture, particularly in the fortified capital of Fira. The Ottomans left their mark as well, reflected in the mosques and the strong culinary influences in Santorini's cuisine.

A Paradise for the Senses: Santorini's Allure

Santorini is a haven for those seeking a sensory adventure. The dazzling sunsets, a fiery spectacle of orange, pink, and purple hues painting the sky, are legendary. The whitewashed houses with their contrasting blue domes create a picture-perfect postcard scene. The scent of lavender and wildflowers in the air mingles with the salty tang of the sea.

Santorini's culinary scene is a delectable blend of Greek and Mediterranean influences. Fresh seafood caught daily stars on menus, complemented by local sun-ripened vegetables, creamy cheeses, and of course, the island's unique wines. Don't miss the chance to savor fava bean puree, a Santorini specialty, or indulge in a traditional Greek yogurt topped with honey and nuts.

Beyond the Tourist Trail: Unveiling Santorini's Hidden Gems

While the caldera villages of Fira and Oia are undeniably captivating, venturing beyond the tourist trail unlocks Santorini's hidden treasures. Explore the charming villages of Megalochori and Pyrgos, with their maze-like alleys and traditional architecture. Hike the trails along the caldera rim for breathtaking panoramic views. Seek out secluded beaches like Vourvoulos or Koloumbos for a tranquil escape.

A Timeless Enchantment: Awaiting You in Santorini

Santorini is an island that captivates the soul. It's a place where the dramatic beauty of nature intertwines with a rich history, offering something for every traveler. Whether you seek adventure, relaxation, cultural immersion, or simply a romantic escape, Santorini awaits to weave its magic on you.

Santorini's Enchantment: A Tapestry Woven with Volcanic Fire and Timeless Beauty

Santorini isn't your average Greek island paradise. Sure, it boasts sun-drenched beaches and charming whitewashed villages, but beneath this postcard-perfect veneer lies a story sculpted by volcanic fury and a unique geological marvel that sets it apart. Here, we delve into the essence of Santorini, highlighting the features that make it a truly unforgettable destination.

Dramatic Caldera: A Legacy of Cataclysmic Change

The centerpiece of Santorini is undoubtedly the caldera, a crescent-shaped body of water embraced by dramatic cliffs that rise hundreds of meters from the sea. This breathtaking landscape wasn't always present. Roughly 3,600 years ago, a massive volcanic eruption ripped through the center of the island, causing the central portion to collapse and leaving behind the now-iconic caldera. This cataclysmic event not only reshaped the island's physical geography but also holds the potential key to the legend of Atlantis.

Today, the caldera is a living testament to Santorini's fiery past. The water shimmers in an array of turquoise hues, a stark contrast to the volcanic cliffs that rise majestically from its edge. Boat tours traverse its surface, allowing visitors to peer into the heart of the volcano through steaming fumaroles on Nea Kameni and Palea Kameni, volcanic islets within the caldera. These islands offer a surreal landscape of volcanic rock formations, and some tours even provide the opportunity for a mud bath in the sulfur springs – a spa experience unlike any other.

Volcanic Tapestry: From Dramatic Cliffs to Unique Wines

Santorini's volcanic heritage extends far beyond the caldera. The volcanic soil that blankets the island imbues the landscape with a unique character. The eastern slopes, gentler than the caldera cliffs, are carpeted with vineyards that produce some of Greece's most intriguing wines. The volcanic ash imparts a distinctive minerality to the grapes, resulting in crisp whites like Assyrtiko, known for its refreshing acidity and citrus notes, and robust reds like Mavrotragano, boasting a complex flavor profile.

The volcanic influence even extends to the island's beaches. Forget the usual white sand – here, you'll find a spectrum of colors: dramatic black sand beaches like Perissa and Kamari, formed from volcanic ash; the Red Beach, a striking geological marvel where red lava pebbles and cliffs create a breathtaking spectacle; and even the White Beach, a hidden gem with pristine white sand offering a serene escape.

Unearthing the Past: A Glimpse into Santorini's History

Santorini's story goes far beyond the volcanic eruption. Excavations at Akrotiri, a Minoan settlement buried by volcanic ash millennia ago, have unearthed a remarkably well-preserved town. Imagine walking amidst multi-story buildings, marveling at intricate frescoes adorning the walls, and witnessing the remnants of a sophisticated civilization that thrived here thousands of years before Christ.

The island's history is a tapestry woven with threads of different cultures. Venetian influence is evident in the architecture, particularly in the fortified capital of Fira, while Ottoman rule left its mark on the mosques and the flavors that enrich Santorini's cuisine.

A Feast for the Senses: Santorini's Allure

A visit to Santorini is an experience that engages all the senses. Witnessing the legendary sunsets, a fiery farewell to the day where the sky explodes with vibrant hues of orange, pink, and purple, is a spectacle that leaves a lasting impression. The iconic whitewashed houses with their contrasting blue domes create a picture-perfect scene that seems to jump straight out of a travel brochure. The air itself carries the fragrance of lavender and wildflowers in bloom, mingling with the salty tang of the Aegean Sea.

Santorini's culinary scene is a delectable blend of Greek and Mediterranean influences. The freshest seafood, caught daily by local fishermen, takes center stage on menus alongside sun-ripened vegetables, creamy cheeses, and of course, the island's unique volcanic wines. Savor fava bean puree, a Santorini specialty with a smooth, earthy texture, or indulge in a traditional Greek yogurt topped with honey and nuts – a simple yet satisfying treat.

Beyond the Tourist Trail: Unveiling Santorini's Hidden Gems

While the caldera villages of Fira and Oia undoubtedly command attention with their stunning views, venturing beyond the tourist trail unlocks Santorini's hidden treasures. Explore the charming villages of Megalochori and Pyrgos, with their maze-like alleys and traditional Cycladic architecture, a world away from the bustling crowds. Hiking trails along the caldera rim reward intrepid explorers with breathtaking panoramic views of the island and the Aegean Sea. And for those seeking a secluded escape, pristine beaches like Vourvoulos or Koloumbos offer a haven of tranquility.

Must-see attractions

Here is a list of must-see attractions in Santorini, Greece, with each described in more than 100 words and incorporating images:

The Caldera: Santorini's crown jewel, the caldera is a flooded volcanic crater that forms the dramatic centerpiece of the island. The villages cling to cliffs hundreds of meters high, offering breathtaking views of the turquoise water below. Boat tours are a fantastic way to explore the caldera, allowing you to sail past volcanic islets, swim in hot springs, and witness volcanic activity up close.

Santorini Greece Caldera

Fira (Thera): Fira, the capital of Santorini, is a vibrant town perched on the cliffs overlooking the caldera. Narrow, winding streets lined with whitewashed houses, shops, and restaurants meander through the town. Don't miss getting lost in the maze-like alleys, browsing through the local shops for souvenirs, and stopping at a charming cafe to take in the caldera views. Fira is especially lively in the evenings, with a captivating atmosphere.

Oia is a village on the northern tip of Santorini, famed for its stunning sunsets and picture-perfect beauty. The whitewashed houses with cascading blue-domed roofs clinging to the cliffs create a scene straight out of a postcard. Oia's narrow streets are lined with art galleries, cafes, and restaurants, offering a delightful atmosphere to explore. Be prepared for crowds, especially during peak season, but the mesmerizing sunsets and captivating charm make Oia a must-visit.

Santorini Greece Oia village

  Akrotiri: an ancient Minoan settlement buried by volcanic ash around 1650 BC, offers a glimpse into a civilization that thrived thousands of years ago. Excavations have revealed remarkably well-preserved houses, multi-story buildings, intricate frescoes, and a wealth of artifacts. Walking through the archeological site is a journey back in time, providing a window into Minoan culture and daily life.

The Beaches: Santorini boasts a variety of beaches, each with its unique character. The black sand beaches of

Perissa and Kamari are the most popular, offering a dramatic setting with volcanic black pebbles and clear blue waters. The Red Beach, near Akrotiri, is a geological marvel with red lava pebbles and cliffs creating a striking visual contrast. For those seeking a more secluded escape, beaches like Vourvoulos and Koloumbos offer pristine white sand and a tranquil atmosphere.

Santorini Greece Perissa beach

Nea Kameni and Palea Kameni: These volcanic islets within the caldera are a stark reminder of Santorini's fiery past. Boat tours take visitors to these islands, where you can witness steaming fumaroles, volcanic rock formations, and even take a mud bath in the sulfur springs – a truly unique experience. Nea Kameni is still an active volcano, and the lunar-like landscape provides a glimpse into the heart of the volcano.

Wine Tasting: Santorini is renowned for its distinctive volcanic wines, produced from grapes grown in the fertile volcanic soil. The island boasts numerous wineries, many with charming settings and breathtaking views. Sample the unique white varietal Assyrtiko, known for its crisp acidity and minerality, or explore the robust reds like Mavrotragano. Wine tasting tours are a delightful way to discover the island's unique wines and learn about the winemaking process.

23

Hiking: Santorini's dramatic cliffs and caldera rim offer fantastic hiking trails for those seeking outdoor adventure. The trail from Fira to Oia is a popular route, providing stunning panoramic views along the way. The hike from Skaros Rock to Oia rewards explorers with breathtaking vistas of the caldera and the Aegean Sea. For a more challenging hike, explore the trails along the volcano rim near Akrotiri.

Sunset in Oia: Witnessing the sunset in Oia is an experience that shouldn't be missed. As the sun dips below the horizon, the sky explodes in a vibrant array of colors, painting the caldera and the whitewashed houses with hues of orange, pink, and purple. Finding a spot along the caldera rim in Oia and soaking in this mesmerizing spectacle is a quintessential Santorini experience.

In addition to these must-see attractions, consider venturing beyond the tourist trail and exploring the charming villages of Megalochori and Pyrgos, with their traditional Cycladic architecture and laid-back atmosphere. Santorini offers something for everyone, from dramatic landscapes and historical sites to culinary delights and outdoor activities. This unique island beckons you to explore its volcanic heritage, captivating beauty, and timeless charm.

The overall vibe.

Santorini exudes a unique vibe that blends elements of romance, adventure, and cultural immersion. Here's a breakdown of the overall atmosphere you can expect:

Romance and Beauty: Santorini is a dream destination for couples seeking a romantic escape. The dramatic scenery, with its iconic whitewashed houses cascading down cliffs overlooking the turquoise caldera, creates a picture-perfect backdrop. Sunsets here are legendary, transforming the sky into a canvas of fiery hues that paint the landscape in a magical glow. Charming cafes with caldera views and intimate restaurants tucked away in narrow alleys provide the perfect ambience for a romantic evening. Whether you're strolling hand-in-hand along the caldera rim or soaking in the serenity of a secluded beach, Santorini's atmosphere is undeniably captivating for couples.

Adventure and Exploration: Beyond the romance, Santorini offers a spirit of adventure for those seeking to delve deeper. Hike along the caldera rim, taking in the breathtaking panoramic views and feeling the invigorating Aegean breeze. Explore the volcanic islets of Nea Kameni and Palea Kameni, where you can witness the raw power of nature through steaming vents and volcanic rock formations. Unearth the secrets of the past at Akrotiri, an ancient Minoan settlement frozen in time. Sailing tours around the caldera offer a chance to swim in hot springs and hidden coves, while exploring hidden beaches like Vourvoulos or Koloumbos provides a sense of discovery. Santorini caters to the adventurous spirit with its unique landscapes and exciting activities.

Cultural Immersion: Santorini's rich history whispers through its cobbled streets and traditional architecture. The island's character reflects the influences of various cultures that have left their mark over time. Explore the charming villages like Megalochori and Pyrgos, where time seems to slow down and traditional Cycladic life unfolds. Delve into the Minoan past at Akrotiri or admire the Venetian architecture in Fira. Savor the island's unique cuisine, where fresh seafood, sun-ripened vegetables, and volcanic wines create a delightful fusion of Greek and Mediterranean flavors. Engaging with the locals, their warm hospitality, and their way of life adds another layer to the cultural immersion experience.

Lively Yet Relaxing: Santorini offers a wonderful balance between lively energy and serene relaxation. The caldera villages of Fira and Oia, particularly during peak season, pulsate with a vibrant atmosphere. Restaurants with caldera views bustle with activity, cafes spill out onto charming squares, and shops overflow with local treasures. However, you can also find pockets of tranquility. Secluded beaches offer a chance to unwind amidst pristine surroundings. Traditional villages away from the main tourist areas exude a laid-back charm, perfect for slowing down and soaking in the relaxed atmosphere.

Santorini's overall vibe is a beautiful tapestry woven with these elements. Whether you seek romance under mesmerizing sunsets, adventure amidst volcanic landscapes, or cultural immersion in a place steeped in history, Santorini has something to offer everyone.

Chapter 2: When to Go

Best time to visit based on whether, crowd and budget

Sun-Kissed Santorini: Peak Season (June-September)

Weather: This is the golden period for weather in Santorini. Imagine basking under the glorious Aegean sun with average temperatures soaring into the high 20s°C (low 80s°F), perfect for swimming in the crystal-clear turquoise waters, indulging in water sports, and exploring the island without breaking a sweat. The skies are predominantly clear, offering uninterrupted sunshine for those picture-perfect postcard moments. However, with the sun comes heat, so be sure to pack sunscreen, sunglasses, and a hat.

Crowds: Be prepared for Santorini at its most bustling. Fira, Oia, and popular beaches like Kamari and Perissa transform into vibrant hives of activity. Expect long lines at restaurants and attractions, especially during peak hours. Navigating the narrow streets and finding a secluded spot on the beach might require some patience. Booking accommodation and activities well in advance is crucial, as availability shrinks rapidly.

Budget: This is the time when Santorini commands a premium. Flights, accommodation, tours, and dining will be at their most expensive. If you're on a tight budget, consider the shoulder seasons or even the winter months.

Bonus: Witnessing the legendary sunsets of Santorini during peak season is an experience in itself. The fiery spectacle of orange, pink, and purple hues painting the sky as the sun dips below the caldera rim is a breathtaking sight that draws crowds for a reason.

Shoulder Seasons: Finding the Sweet Spot (April-May & October-November)

Weather: These shoulder months offer a delightful balance between pleasant weather and manageable crowds. Temperatures hover in the comfortable mid-20s°C (mid-70s°F), making sightseeing and outdoor activities enjoyable without the scorching summer heat. You might encounter occasional rain showers, but they are usually brief and refresh the landscape. The Aegean Sea remains inviting for swimming, although the water might not be as warm as peak season.

Crowds: Compared to the peak season, the shoulder months offer a noticeable respite from the throngs of tourists. You'll still find crowds at popular attractions, but the overall atmosphere is less congested, allowing you to explore at a more leisurely pace and potentially snag better deals on last-minute accommodation.

Budget: Accommodation and activity prices start to dip compared to peak season. You might find some good deals, especially towards the beginning or end of the shoulder seasons. With a little planning and flexibility, you can experience Santorini's charm without breaking the bank.

Bonus: Witnessing the "blooming" of Santorini during the shoulder seasons is a hidden gem. The volcanic slopes come alive with vibrant wildflowers, adding a touch of color to the dramatic landscape. The island also hosts several festivals during these months, like the Easter celebrations or the Tomato Festival in Santorini (usually held in late August or early September), offering a glimpse into local traditions.

Budget-Conscious Santorini: Winter Escapade (December-March)

Weather: Winter in Santorini is mild with cooler temperatures, averaging in the mid-teens°C (low 60s°F). This might not be ideal for swimming or sunbathing, but the island takes on a unique charm during this time. Imagine strolling through the caldera villages under crisp winter skies or witnessing the dramatic cliffs dusted with a light snow (a rare occurrence). However, be prepared for occasional rain and strong winds that can sometimes whip across the caldera. Some restaurants and shops may have limited hours or be closed entirely.

Crowds: The island experiences the fewest crowds during the winter months. Popular tourist spots will be noticeably quieter, offering a more secluded and peaceful experience. If you prefer a more intimate exploration of Santorini's beauty and rich history, winter might be the perfect time for you.

Budget: This is the most budget-friendly time to visit Santorini. Flights and accommodations plummet in price, making it a great option for travelers on a tight budget. You might even find some incredible deals on last-minute getaways.

Bonus: Witnessing the caldera bathed in the soft glow of winter light is a sight to behold. The absence of crowds allows you to truly appreciate the dramatic beauty of the island's landscape without feeling rushed. Winter is also a good time to delve into the island's culinary scene. Cozy tavernas with fireplaces offer the perfect setting to savor traditional Santorini dishes and local wines.

Unveiling Santorini's Charm: Beyond the Peak Season Rush

Santorini's allure transcends the typical summer frenzy. While the peak season (June-September) boasts glorious sunshine and vibrant activity, it also comes with crowds and premium prices. For travelers seeking a more balanced experience, the shoulder seasons (April-May & October-November) and even the off-season (December-March) offer a unique perspective on this captivating island.

Shoulder Seasons: A Symphony of Comfort and Beauty (April-May & October-November)

Weather: Imagine exploring Santorini bathed in a warm, golden light. The shoulder seasons offer pleasant temperatures in the mid-20s°C (mid-70s°F), perfect for sightseeing and outdoor activities without the oppressive summer heat. The Aegean Sea remains inviting for swimming, although the water might not be as balmy as peak season. Occasional rain showers can freshen the landscape, adding a touch of drama to the already stunning vistas.

Crowds: Shoulder seasons offer a significant respite from the peak season throngs. Popular attractions like Fira and Oia will still have visitors, but the overall atmosphere is less congested. You'll encounter shorter lines at restaurants and attractions, allowing you to explore at a more leisurely pace and truly immerse yourself in the island's beauty.

Budget: Accommodation and activity prices start to dip compared to peak season. With a little planning and flexibility, you can experience Santorini's charm without breaking the bank. Early bookings during the shoulder seasons can yield significant savings, allowing you to splurge on a unique experience like a private catamaran tour or a gourmet dining experience.

Beyond the Basics: Unveiling Shoulder Season Gems

Blooming Landscapes: Witnessing the "blooming" of Santorini during the shoulder seasons is a hidden treasure. The volcanic slopes transform into a vibrant tapestry of wildflowers, adding a touch of color to the dramatic scenery. Imagine capturing photos of whitewashed houses cascading down cliffs against a backdrop of wildflowers in full bloom – a sight exclusive to the shoulder seasons.

Festivals and Events: The shoulder seasons come alive with vibrant celebrations. Easter, a major religious festival in Greece, is observed with great fanfare in Santorini. Processions, special church services, and traditional feasts fill the island with a festive atmosphere.

The Tomato Festival, usually held in late August or early September, is another unique experience. Celebrate the island's agricultural heritage with tomato-themed dishes, cooking demonstrations, and lively music.

Hiking Paradise: The shoulder seasons offer ideal conditions for exploring Santorini's many hiking trails. The cooler temperatures make traversing the volcanic terrain more enjoyable. Imagine traversing the path from Fira to Oia, taking in breathtaking panoramic views of the caldera without battling the summer heat. Explore the trails along the volcano rim near Akrotiri or conquer the challenging hike up Skaros Rock for unparalleled vistas of the island and the Aegean Sea.

Off-Season Escapade: Santorini Unveiled (December-March)

Weather: Winter in Santorini casts a unique spell. Temperatures average in the mid-teens°C (low 60s°F), making it less ideal for swimming or sunbathing but offering a different perspective on the island. Imagine strolling through the caldera villages under crisp winter skies or witnessing the dramatic cliffs dusted with a light snow (a rare occurrence). Be prepared for occasional rain and strong winds that can sometimes whip across the caldera. Some restaurants and shops may have limited hours or be closed entirely.

Crowds: The island experiences the fewest crowds during the winter months. Popular tourist spots will be noticeably quieter, offering a more secluded and peaceful experience. If you prefer a more intimate exploration of Santorini's historical sites and hidden gems, the off-season might be the perfect time for you.

Budget: This is the most budget-friendly time to visit Santorini. Flights and accommodations plummet in price, making it a great option for budget-conscious travelers. You might even find incredible deals on last-minute getaways, allowing you to stretch your travel budget further.

Beyond the Savings: Off-Season Santorini's Allure

Caldera Bathed in Winter Light: Witnessing the caldera bathed in the soft glow of winter light is a sight to behold. The absence of crowds allows you to truly appreciate the dramatic beauty of the island's landscape without feeling rushed. Imagine capturing photos of the caldera with a clear winter sky as your backdrop – a unique perspective that's hard to achieve during peak season.

Culinary Delights by the Fireplace: Winter is a great time to delve into the island's culinary scene. Cozy tavernas with crackling fireplaces offer the perfect setting to savor traditional Santorini dishes and local wines. Imagine indulging in a steaming bowl of food.

Chapter 3: Budgeting for Santorini

Conquering Santorini: A Guide to Budget-Friendly Travel

Santorini beckons with its dramatic cliffs, charming villages, and legendary sunsets. But fear not, budget-conscious travelers! With careful planning and these handy tips, you can experience the magic of Santorini without breaking the bank. Here's a comprehensive guide to creating a budget for your Santorini adventure, covering flights, accommodation, food, activities, and transportation.

Flights: Soaring on a Budget

Track and Book Smart: Utilize flight comparison websites like Google Flights, Kayak, or Skyscanner to track airfare fluctuations. Set price alerts and book your flights during off-peak seasons (April-May & October-November) or even the winter months (December-March) for the most significant savings.

Consider alternative airports: While Santorini (JTR) is the main airport, explore flights to nearby islands like Crete (HER) or Athens (ATH). Sometimes, flying into a different airport and then taking a ferry to Santorini can be cheaper, especially if you factor in baggage fees and travel time.

Accommodation: Finding Your Cozy Santorini Haven

Embrace the Shoulder Seasons: Hotels and vacation rentals significantly reduce their rates during the shoulder seasons. Aim for bookings outside the peak summer months (June-September) to score the best deals.

Explore Alternative Locations: While Fira and Oia are undeniably charming, consider staying in villages like Megalochori, Pyrgos, or Kamari. These offer a more relaxed atmosphere and often have lower accommodation costs while still providing easy access to the island's highlights.

Consider Apartment Rentals: For longer stays or those traveling in groups, apartment rentals on platforms like Airbnb can be a budget-friendly option. Having access to a kitchen allows you to prepare some meals, further reducing your food expenses.

Food: A Culinary Adventure Without Breaking the Bank

Embrace Local Markets: Venture into local farmers' markets to stock up on fresh, seasonal produce at unbeatable prices. Imagine whipping up a delicious Greek salad with sun-ripened tomatoes, crisp cucumbers, and creamy feta cheese, all sourced from the market.

Dine Beyond the Caldera Views: Restaurants with caldera views often come with a premium price tag. Explore tavernas tucked away in the backstreets; they often offer a more authentic dining experience with delicious local dishes at reasonable prices.

Sample Street Food: Don't miss out on Santorini's street food scene. Gyros, souvlaki, and fresh seafood wraps are delicious and affordable options for a quick lunch or a casual dinner.

Embrace Self-Catering: Stock up on groceries and prepare some meals in your accommodation. This doesn't have to be elaborate; think simple pasta dishes, Greek salads, or sandwiches with local cheeses and olives.

Activities: Experiencing Santorini's Magic Affordably

Free Walking Tours: Several companies offer free walking tours of Fira and Oia. These tours are a fantastic way to learn about Santorini's history, culture, and hidden gems while keeping costs down. Remember to tip your guide if you enjoyed the tour.

Public Transportation: The local bus network is a convenient and affordable way to get around the island. Purchase a pass for multiple journeys to save even more. While taxis are available, they tend to be more expensive.

Explore Free Sites: Santorini boasts several free historical sites to explore. Akrotiri, the ancient Minoan settlement, offers a glimpse into a civilization frozen in time. The charming villages like Megalochori and Pyrgos are free to wander through, soaking in their traditional Cycladic architecture.

Prioritize Experiences: Instead of cramming in every activity, choose a few experiences that truly resonate with you. Consider hiking the caldera rim for breathtaking views, swimming in hidden coves, or participating in a wine tasting tour at a local winery.

Transportation: Navigating Santorini on a Budget

Utilize the Bus Network: The local bus network is a convenient and affordable way to get around the island. Purchase a multi-day pass to save money on individual fares.

Walking Whenever Possible: Santorini is a relatively small island, and many villages are pedestrian-friendly. Walking between Fira and Firostefani, exploring the charming alleys of Oia, or strolling along the Kamari beachfront are great ways to experience the island's beauty while saving on transportation costs.

Consider Ferry Options: Ferry rides from Santorini to nearby islands like Naxos, Ios, or Mykonos can be a fun and affordable way to spend a day trip. Compare ferry schedules and prices to find the best deals.

Remember: Budgeting for travel is an ongoing process. Throughout your trip

Santorini on a Budget: High Season vs. Low Season Costs

Santorini's dramatic beauty and captivating atmosphere come at a price, but that price tag can fluctuate significantly depending on the season you choose to visit. Here's a breakdown of the high season (June-September) vs. low season (December-March) costs for flights, accommodation, food, activities, and transportation, helping you decide which time best suits your budget.

High Season (June-September): Prepare for a Premium Experience

Flights: Buckle up for the most expensive time to fly to Santorini. Airlines know demand is high and adjust prices accordingly. Expect to pay double or even triple the cost of flights compared to the shoulder seasons or off-season.

Accommodation: Hotels and vacation rentals reach their peak pricing during this period. Popular locations like Fira and Oia will see the most significant hikes. Booking well in advance is crucial, as availability shrinks quickly.

Food: Restaurants, especially those with caldera views, inflate their prices during peak season. While the quality and variety remain excellent, be prepared to pay a premium for your meals.

Example: High Season Costs

Flights: Roundtrip flight from New York (JFK) to Santorini (JTR) - $1,500 - $2,000

Accommodation: Double room with a caldera view in Fira - $400 - $600 per night

Dinner for two at a restaurant with a caldera view: $100 - $150

Low Season (December-March): Santorini Unveiled on a Budget

Flights: Low season is the time to snag incredible flight deals. You might find fares that are 50-70% cheaper compared to peak season, making Santorini a much more affordable destination.

Accommodation: Hotels and vacation rentals significantly reduce their rates during the winter months. You might find luxurious accommodations at a fraction of their peak season price.

Food: Restaurants adjust their prices to reflect the lower tourist volume. Enjoy delicious meals at tavernas without breaking the bank.

45

Example: Low Season Costs

Flights: Roundtrip flight from New York (JFK) to Santorini (JTR) - $500 - $700

Accommodation: Double room with a caldera view in Fira - $150 - $250 per night

Dinner for two at a restaurant with a caldera view: $50 - $70

Beyond the Price Tag: High Season vs. Low Season Considerations

High Season:

Crowds: Be prepared for peak season crowds. Popular attractions like Fira, Oia, and beaches like Kamari will be bustling with activity. Finding a secluded spot on the beach or navigating narrow streets might require patience. Booking tours and activities in advance is recommended.

Weather: glorious sunshine, warm temperatures averaging in the high 20s°C (low 80s°F), and calm seas. Perfect for swimming, sunbathing, and enjoying outdoor activities. However, the heat can be intense, especially for those not accustomed to it.

Limited Availability: Accommodation and activity options fill up quickly during peak season. Booking well in advance is crucial to secure your preferred choices.

Low Season:

Weather: Milder temperatures, averaging in the mid-teens°C (low 60s°F) with occasional rain showers. The Aegean Sea might be too cool for swimming for some travelers. However, the island takes on a unique charm with fewer crowds and the possibility of witnessing snow on the cliffs (a rare occurrence).

Limited Options: Some restaurants and shops might have limited hours or be closed entirely during the winter months.

Peace and Tranquility: Enjoy a more peaceful and secluded experience with significantly fewer crowds. Explore the island's beauty and historical sites at your own pace.

Ultimately, the best time to visit Santorini depends on your priorities.

For budget-conscious travelers: The low season (December-March) offers the most affordable option with significantly lower flight and accommodation costs.

For sun seekers and those who love vibrant atmospheres: The high season (June-September) boasts glorious weather, perfect for swimming and enjoying outdoor activities.

For a balance between affordability and pleasant weather: Consider the shoulder seasons (April-May & October-November) when crowds start to thin out, and prices become more reasonable.

Remember: With some flexibility and planning, you can experience the magic of Santorini at a price that suits your budget.

Chapter 4: Visas and Entry Requirements:

Navigating the Greek Gateway: A Comprehensive Guide to Visa Requirements

Greece, the cradle of democracy and a land steeped in mythology, beckons travelers with its ancient ruins, pristine beaches, and vibrant culture. However, before embarking on your Greek odyssey, understanding the visa requirements is crucial. This guide provides a detailed breakdown of visa needs for various nationalities, ensuring a smooth entry process.

Visa-Free Entry: Exploring Greece with Ease

The good news is that a significant number of countries enjoy visa-free access to Greece. These nations are part of the Schengen Area, a zone comprising 26 European countries that have agreed on standardized visa policies. Here's a breakdown of who can enter Greece visa-free:

European Union (EU) Citizens and European Economic Area (EEA) Nationals: EU citizens and nationals of Iceland, Liechtenstein, Norway, and Switzerland can travel freely within the Schengen Area, including Greece, for up to 90 days in any 180-day period without a visa. A valid passport is all that's required.

Schengen Associated Countries: Andorra, Monaco, San Marino, and Vatican City also enjoy visa-free access to Greece under their association agreements with the Schengen Area. Citizens of these countries can visit Greece for up to 90 days within a 180-day period with a valid passport.

Visa-Free Agreements: Greece has bilateral visa-free agreements with a multitude of countries. Citizens of these countries can enter Greece for tourism or business purposes for a specific duration without a visa, typically up to 90 days. Always double-check the latest information from the Greek Ministry of Foreign Affairs or the nearest Greek embassy/consulate in your home country for the most up-to-date list and any specific requirements, such as reciprocity fees.

Examples of countries with Visa-Free Agreements with Greece (not an exhaustive list):
- United States
- Canada
- Australia,

- New Zealand
- United Kingdom (until the UK's withdrawal from the European Union is fully finalized)
- Japan
- South Korea
- Singapore
- Many South American countries

Entering the Realm of Visas: Understanding the Process

If your country is not on the visa-free list, don't fret! Greece offers various visa categories to cater to different travel purposes. Here's a glimpse into the most common types of visas:

Schengen Tourist Visa: This visa is ideal for short-term stays in Greece, typically up to 90 days. It allows you to visit not only Greece but also other Schengen Area countries during your designated travel period. Documents required typically include a completed visa application form, a valid passport, passport-sized photos, proof of travel and accommodation, proof of sufficient financial means for your stay, and travel medical insurance. Processing times can vary, so apply well in advance of your trip.

National Visa (Long-Term Stay): For stays exceeding 90 days or for purposes other than tourism (e.g., studying, working), you'll need a National Visa. The specific requirements and application procedures will vary depending on the visa type (work, study, research etc.). Contact the nearest Greek embassy/consulate in your home country for detailed information and guidance.

Important Considerations for Visa Applications:

Validity of Travel Documents: Ensure your passport has at least six months of validity remaining from your planned date of entry into Greece and sufficient blank pages for visa stamps.

Travel Medical Insurance: Most visa applications require proof of travel medical insurance with a minimum coverage amount (usually €30,000) that is valid throughout the Schengen Area.

Application Fees: Be prepared to pay visa application fees, which can vary depending on your nationality and visa type. These fees are typically non-refundable, even if your visa application is denied.

Processing Times: Visa processing times can vary depending on your nationality, the workload of the embassy/consulate, and the complexity of your application. Plan accordingly, and submit your application well in advance of your intended travel date.

Embassy and Consulate Information:

The Greek Ministry of Foreign Affairs website provides a comprehensive list of Greek embassies and consulates worldwide: https://www.mfa.gr/missionsabroad/en/

Remember: Visa requirements can change, so it's crucial to obtain the latest information from official sources before your trip. Contact the nearest Greek embassy/consulate or visit the Ministry of Foreign Affairs website for the most up-to-date details.

By familiarizing yourself with the visa requirements, you can ensure a smooth entry process and embark on your Greek adventure with peace of mind. Safe travels!

A Meticulous Guide to Visa Requirements and Pre-Travel Preparations

Greece, the land of ancient myths, turquoise waters, and delectable cuisine, beckons travelers worldwide. But before you set sail on your Greek odyssey, navigating visa requirements and pre-travel registrations is essential. This elaborate guide equips you with the knowledge to ensure a smooth entry process and a memorable Greek adventure.

Understanding Visa Exemptions: Exploring Greece with Ease

The good news for many travelers is that Greece participates in the Schengen Area, a zone of 26 European countries with standardized visa policies. If you hail from one of the following categories, you might be fortunate enough to enter Greece visa-free:

European Union (EU) Citizens and European Economic Area (EEA) Nationals: EU citizens and nationals of Iceland, Liechtenstein, Norway, and Switzerland can travel freely within the Schengen Area, including Greece, for up to 90 days in any 180-day period without a visa. All they need is a valid passport.

Schengen Associated Countries: Andorra, Monaco, San Marino, and Vatican City also enjoy visa-free access to Greece under their association agreements with the Schengen Area. Citizens of these countries can visit Greece for up to 90 days within a 180-day period with a valid passport.

Visa-Free Agreements: Greece has bilateral visa-free agreements with many countries. Citizens of these countries can enter Greece for tourism or business purposes for a specific duration, typically up to 90 days, without a visa. Always double-check the latest information from the Greek Ministry of Foreign Affairs or the nearest Greek embassy/consulate in your home country for the most up-to-date list and any specific requirements, such as reciprocity fees.

Examples of Countries with Visa-Free Agreements with Greece (not an exhaustive list):
- United States
- Canada
- Australia
- New Zealand
- United Kingdom (until the UK's withdrawal from the European Union is fully finalized)
- Japan
- South Korea
- Singapore
- Many South American countries

Necessary Documents for Visa-Free Entry (Even if you don't require a visa, having these documents handy can expedite the entry process):

Valid Passport: Ensure your passport has at least six months of validity remaining from your planned date of entry into Greece. It should also have sufficient blank pages for any entry stamps you might receive.

Proof of Onward or Return Travel: Greek immigration officials might request proof that you have a departing flight or ferry ticket out of Greece, so have this documentation readily available.

Proof of Sufficient Funds: While not always mandatory, having documents that demonstrate you have sufficient financial resources to support yourself during your stay in Greece can be helpful. This could include bank statements, credit cards, or traveler's checks.

Pre-Travel Registration Requirements (While not mandatory for all nationalities, some countries may require pre-registration):

United States Electronic System for Travel Authorization (ESTA): U.S. citizens do not need a visa for stays up to 90 days in Greece. However, they must obtain an ESTA authorization prior to travel. This online application is usually quick and straightforward.

United Kingdom Electronic Travel Authorization (ETA): British citizens traveling to Greece after Brexit might require an ETA depending on the outcome of ongoing negotiations between Greece and the UK. Stay updated on the latest requirements by checking the UK government's travel advice for Greece or the Greek Ministry of Foreign Affairs website.

Entering the Realm of Visas: Understanding the Process

If your country is not on the visa-free list, fret not! Greece offers various visa categories to cater to different travel purposes. Here's a glimpse into the most common types of visas and the documents you'll typically need to prepare:

Schengen Tourist Visa: Ideal for short-term stays in Greece, typically up to 90 days. This visa allows you to visit not only Greece but also other Schengen Area countries during your designated travel period. Here's what you'll usually need:

Completed Visa Application Form: The application form can be downloaded from the website of the Greek embassy/consulate in your home country. Fill it out accurately and completely.

Valid Passport: As mentioned earlier, your passport should have at least six months of validity remaining and sufficient blank pages.

Passport-Sized Photos: Two recent passport-sized photos meeting the specified requirements (size, background color, etc.) are typically required.

Proof of Travel and Accommodation: This could include a printout of your flight itinerary or ferry tickets and hotel reservation confirmations.

Chapter 5: Getting There:

Reaching the Shores of Santorini: A Guide to Flights and Ferries

Santorini, with its dramatic cliffs, whitewashed villages, and captivating sunsets, beckons travelers from all corners of the globe. But how do you reach this volcanic paradise? Fear not, for this guide explores both flying and taking ferries to Santorini, equipping you with the knowledge to choose the best option for your travel style and budget.

Soaring to Santorini: A Bird's Eye View Approach

Direct Flights: If time is of the essence or you prefer a faster option, direct flights are the way to go. Several airlines offer seasonal direct flights to Santorini (JTR) from major international hubs, particularly during peak season (June-September). The flight duration varies depending on your departure location, but expect it to be between 2-6 hours from major European cities.

Pros: Fastest travel option, convenient for long distances, comfortable seating arrangements (depending on your class).

Cons: Generally more expensive than ferries, limited availability and higher prices during peak season.

Tips for Booking Flights:

Book in Advance: Especially during peak season, flights to Santorini fill up quickly. Booking well in advance (3-6 months) can help you secure better deals.

Consider Alternative Airports: While Santorini has its own airport (JTR), explore flying into nearby islands like Crete (HER) or Athens (ATH) and then taking a connecting ferry to Santorini. Sometimes, this combination can be cheaper, especially if you factor in baggage fees.

Track Flight Prices: Utilize flight comparison websites like Google Flights, Kayak, or Skyscanner to track price fluctuations and book your flights when prices dip.

Sailing the Aegean: A Ferry Odyssey to Santorini

Ferry Routes: Ferries are a popular and scenic way to reach Santorini, offering a more relaxed travel experience. Several ferry companies operate routes from mainland Greece (Piraeus port near Athens) and nearby islands like Mykonos, Naxos, Ios, and Crete. The journey time varies depending on the ferry type (high-speed vs. conventional) and your departure point. Expect ferry rides from Athens to take between 5-8 hours, while island hopping between Santorini and neighboring islands can take anywhere from 30 minutes to 2 hours.

Pros: Scenic journey through the Aegean Sea, multiple departure points offering flexibility, often more affordable than flights during shoulder seasons and off-season.

Cons: Generally slower than flying, can be susceptible to weather delays or cancellations, limited cabin availability during peak season.

Types of Ferries:

High-Speed Ferries: These ferries offer the fastest travel time but come at a premium price. They are ideal if you're short on time or want a more comfortable journey.

Conventional Ferries: These ferries are a more budget-friendly option and take longer than high-speed ferries. They offer basic amenities like seating areas and sometimes cafes or restaurants onboard.

61

Car Ferries: If you're traveling with a car or motorbike, these ferries allow you to bring your vehicle onboard for a fee.

Tips for Booking Ferries:

Book in Advance: During peak season (June-September), ferry tickets can sell out, especially on popular routes. Book your tickets well in advance to secure your desired date and time.

Compare Prices and Schedules: Several ferry companies operate between various ports. Utilize ferry comparison websites or ferry company websites to compare prices, schedules, and amenities to find the best option for your needs.

Consider Island Hopping: If you plan to visit multiple Greek islands, consider incorporating Santorini into your itinerary. Ferries provide a convenient way to travel between islands, adding a touch of adventure to your Greek adventure.

Ultimately, the choice between flying and taking a ferry to Santorini depends on your priorities:

For Speed and Convenience: Flying might be the better option, especially if you're traveling long distances or have limited time.

For Budget and Scenic Experience: Ferries offer a more affordable and scenic way to reach Santorini, particularly during the shoulder seasons and off-season.

For Island Hopping: Ferries are the ideal choice if you plan on exploring multiple Greek islands during your trip.

So, pack your bags, choose your mode of transportation, and prepare to be captivated by the magic of Santorini!

Unveiling Santorini: A Guide to Reaching Paradise from Afar

Santorini, a crown jewel of Greece, entices travelers with its dramatic volcanic cliffs, sugar-cube houses clinging to the caldera, and legendary sunsets. But for those venturing from afar, like the United States, navigating the logistics of getting there can be a puzzle. Fear not, intrepid explorer! This comprehensive guide explores your travel options from various origins, including the US, outlining estimated travel times and providing valuable booking tips to help you score the best deals on your Aegean adventure.

Taking Flight to Santorini: Crossing the Atlantic

Direct Flights (Seasonal): During peak travel season (June-September), some airlines offer coveted direct flights from major US hubs like New York (JFK), Newark (EWR), Chicago (ORD), and Los Angeles (LAX) to Santorini (JTR). These flights are the fastest option, whisking you away in 10-14 hours, depending on your departure city. However, be prepared for premium prices, particularly for last-minute bookings.

Connecting Flights: A more common and budget-friendly option is to fly into Athens International Airport (ATH) with a connecting flight to Santorini. Major airlines offer frequent connections throughout the year, making this a readily available choice. The total travel time, including layovers in major European hubs like Frankfurt (FRA) or Paris (CDG), can range from 14-20 hours.

Booking Tips for Flights:

Plan Ahead: For the best deals, particularly on direct flights, aim to book your tickets 3-6 months in advance, especially during peak season.

Consider Alternative Routes: Explore flying into nearby islands like Crete (HER) or Mykonos (JMK) with a connecting ferry to Santorini. This option can sometimes be more budget-friendly, especially if you find deals on flights to these islands.

Utilize Flight Comparison Tools: Websites like Google Flights, Kayak, or Skyscanner are your allies. Set price alerts for your desired route and track price fluctuations. These tools can notify you when prices drop, allowing you to book when the deals are hot.

Consider Shoulder Seasons: If you have flexibility, target shoulder seasons (April-May & October-November) when flight prices typically dip compared to peak season.

Sailing the Aegean: A Ferry Odyssey from Athens

Ferry from Athens (Piraeus Port): For a more relaxed and scenic travel experience, consider taking a ferry from Athens to Santorini. This journey allows you to soak in the beauty of the Aegean Sea, dotted with charming islands and sapphire-colored waters. High-speed ferries complete the journey in approximately 5-8 hours, while conventional ferries offer a more budget-friendly option with a longer travel time (around 8-12 hours).

Island Hopping: If you plan to explore other Greek islands like Mykonos, Naxos, or Ios, ferries provide the ultimate flexibility. You can create a multi-stop itinerary, hopping from island to island at your own pace.

Booking Tips for Ferries:

Book in Advance: During peak season, ferries can sell out, especially on popular routes like Athens-Santorini. Book your tickets well in advance (2-3 months) to secure your desired date and time.

Compare Prices and Schedules: Several ferry companies operate between Piraeus port and Santorini. Use ferry comparison websites like Ferryhopper or DirectFerries.com, or visit the websites of individual ferry companies (e.g., SeaJets, Hellenic Seaways, Minoan Lines) to compare prices, schedules, and amenities offered by different ferries (e.g., high-speed vs. conventional, cabin options).

Estimated Travel Times from Various Origins (including layovers):
United States (Major Cities):

- New York (JFK) to Santorini (JTR): 14-18 hours (flight)
- Los Angeles (LAX) to Santorini (JTR): 16-20 hours (flight)
- Chicago (ORD) to Santorini (JTR): 15-19 hours (flight)

- o Miami (MIA) to Santorini (JTR): 16-20 hours (flight) with connections in Europe

Europe (Major Cities):

- o London (LHR) to Santorini (JTR): 4-8 hours (flight) with connections
- o Paris (CDG) to Santorini (JTR): 4-8 hours (flight) with connections
- o Frankfurt (FRA) to Santorini (JTR): 4-8 hours (flight) with connections

Santorini Travel Guide 2024 by William F. Peck

Part 2: Accommodations and Logistics

Chapter 6: Where to Stay:

Unveiling Santorini's Stays: A Guide to Choosing Your Ideal Location

Santorini's dramatic landscapes and iconic whitewashed villages present a plethora of accommodation options. But with so many choices, selecting the perfect spot can be overwhelming. Fear not, wanderer! This guide delves into Santorini's most popular areas to stay, considering factors like budget, proximity to attractions, nightlife preferences, and the view you crave (caldera or inland).

Oia (pronounced ee-ah):

Ambiance: Oia is undeniably Santorini's crown jewel. Cobbled streets wind through charming houses boasting breathtaking caldera views. Sunsets here are legendary, attracting photographers and romantics alike.

Budget: Oia is the most expensive area to stay in Santorini. Expect to pay a premium for hotels with caldera views, particularly during peak season.

Proximity to Attractions: Oia boasts its own charm with its traditional architecture, art galleries, and charming shops. The village is a short bus ride from Fira, the island's capital.

Nightlife: While Oia has a few lively bars and restaurants, it's not known for its pulsating nightlife. The focus here is on romantic evenings and soaking in the ambiance.

Views: The majority of hotels in Oia offer stunning caldera views, making it ideal for those who want to wake up to breathtaking panoramas.

Ideal for: Honeymooners, couples seeking romance, photography enthusiasts, those who prioritize caldera views.

Fira (pronounced fee-ra):

Ambiance: Fira, the island's capital, offers a vibrant atmosphere with bustling shops, restaurants, and cafes lining the caldera cliffside. It's a great base for exploring the island.

Budget: Fira offers a wider range of accommodation options compared to Oia, catering to various budgets. You can find luxury hotels with caldera views, charming boutique hotels tucked away in the backstreets, and budget-friendly options further inland.

Proximity to Attractions: Fira is the central hub for buses, taxis, and tours, making it a convenient base for exploring the island's attractions like museums, archaeological sites, and beaches.

Nightlife: Fira is the liveliest spot on the island, with a vibrant nightlife scene. You'll find bars with live music, rooftop terraces overlooking the caldera, and nightclubs catering to different tastes.

Views: Many hotels in Fira offer caldera views, although some are partially obstructed. Inland areas offer a more traditional village experience with limited views.

Ideal for: Travelers seeking a lively atmosphere, those who want a central location for exploring, budget-conscious travelers (with some flexibility based on location and amenities).

Firostefani (pronounced fee-ro-stef-ah-nee):

Ambiance: Firostefani offers a peaceful haven nestled between Fira and Oia. It boasts stunning caldera views with a quieter atmosphere compared to Fira.

71

Budget: Accommodation options in Firostefani fall within a mid-range price bracket, offering a good balance between affordability and amenities.

Proximity to Attractions: Firostefani is within walking distance of Fira and Oia, making it easy to access restaurants, shops, and attractions in both villages.

Nightlife: Firostefani has a few restaurants and bars, but the nightlife scene is more subdued compared to Fira.

Views: The majority of hotels in Firostefani offer stunning caldera views, making it a good option for those seeking breathtaking panoramas without the hustle and bustle of Oia.

Ideal for: Couples seeking a romantic escape with caldera views, travelers who want a central location with a quieter atmosphere, those on a moderate budget.

Imerovigli (pronounced ee-meh-roh-vee-ghee):

Ambiance: Imerovigli is a cliffside village known for its tranquility and breathtaking panoramic views of the caldera. Luxury hotels and infinity pools dominate the landscape.

Budget: Imerovigli is the most expensive area to stay in Santorini after Oia. Expect to pay a premium for luxury accommodations with unparalleled caldera views.

Proximity to Attractions: Imerovigli is a short distance from Fira by bus or taxi. Within the village itself, there are limited restaurants and shops.

Nightlife: Imerovigli boasts a serene ambiance with minimal nightlife options.

Views: Breathtaking, unobstructed caldera views are the highlight of Imerovigli.

Ideal for: Luxury travelers seeking a secluded and romantic escape with the most stunning caldera views.

Chapter 7: Finding the Perfect Accommodation:

Conquering Santorini's Stays: Tips for Finding Your Ideal Accommodation

Santorini's enchanting villages offer a diverse range of accommodation options, from traditional cave houses to luxurious hotels and charming guesthouses. But navigating the plethora of choices can be tricky. Fear not, intrepid explorer! Here are some valuable tips to help you unearth the perfect place to lay your head during your Santorini adventure:

Tailor Your Search:

Budget: Determine your budget upfront. Santorini caters to various budgets, but popular areas like Oia and Imerovigli tend to be pricier.

Location: Consider your priorities. Do you crave caldera views and a vibrant atmosphere (Fira), a romantic escape with tranquility (Firostefani or Imerovigli), or a budget-friendly option further inland?

Travel Style: Are you a couple seeking romance (cave houses!), a group of friends on an adventure (vacation rentals!), or a solo traveler on a budget (hostels or guesthouses)?

Utilize Online Booking Platforms:

Booking.com, Expedia, or Agoda: These popular platforms offer a wide range of accommodation options, allowing you to compare prices, amenities, and guest reviews. Utilize filters to narrow down your search based on location, price range, guest rating, and desired amenities (pool, view, etc.).

Seek Out Boutique Hotels and Local Options:

Small Luxury Hotels of the World (SLH): This website curates a collection of unique and independent hotels, perfect for those seeking a personalized experience and boutique charm.

Search Santorini-Specific Websites: Many local Santorini travel agencies and accommodation providers maintain their own websites. Explore these for unique finds and hidden gems, especially cave houses and traditional guesthouses.

Embrace Cave Houses:

A Unique Santorini Experience: Cave houses, carved into the volcanic cliffs, offer a truly Santorini experience. Many cave houses boast modern amenities while retaining their traditional charm.

Temperature Control: Cave houses are naturally cool in the summer and warm in the winter, making them a great choice year-round.

Filtering by "Cave House" Option: Many booking platforms allow you to filter your search results by "cave house" to find these unique accommodations.

Consider Vacation Rentals:

Perfect for Groups or Families: Vacation rentals offer more space and privacy, ideal for groups or families traveling together. They often come with kitchens, providing flexibility for meals.

Search on VRBO or Airbnb: Popular platforms like VRBO and Airbnb offer a wide range of vacation rental options in Santorini. Read reviews carefully to ensure the rental meets your expectations.

Read Reviews and Ratings:

Guest Insights: Reviews left by previous guests offer valuable insights into the property's location, amenities, cleanliness, and overall atmosphere.

Pay Attention to Details: Read reviews with a critical eye, focusing on aspects like noise levels, proximity to amenities, and the responsiveness of the host (for rentals).

Don't Forget the Power of Negotiation:

Especially During Off-Season: If you're traveling during shoulder seasons or the off-season, consider contacting hotels or guesthouses directly. You might be able to negotiate a better rate, especially for longer stays.

Finally, Book in Advance:

Peak Season Demand: Santorini is a popular destination, especially during peak season (June-September). Book your accommodation well in advance (3-6 months) to secure your desired location and avoid disappointment.

Mastering the Santorini Stay: Booking Platforms and Deal-Scoring Strategies

Santorini's dramatic landscapes and iconic villages come with a variety of stay options, but securing the perfect accommodation at the right price requires strategic planning. Fear not, budget-savvy traveler! This guide equips you with the knowledge to navigate popular booking platforms and resources to unearth the best deals on your Santorini escape.

Booking Platforms: Launching Your Search

MAINSTREAM MONSTERS: Booking.com, Expedia, Agoda - These household names offer a vast selection of Santorini stays, from budget-friendly hostels to luxury cave houses. They excel in:

- Price Comparison: Easily compare prices and amenities across different property types to find the best value for your money.
- Filtering Options: Refine your search based on budget, location, guest rating, amenities (think pool view, balcony etc.), and even property type (hotels, guesthouses, vacation rentals).
- Guest Reviews: Gain valuable insights from past travelers about the property's

cleanliness, location, and overall atmosphere. Read reviews with a critical eye to identify any recurring issues.

Tips for Scoring Deals on Mainstream Platforms:

Play the Dates Game: Santorini's prices fluctuate throughout the season. Consider traveling during shoulder seasons (April-May & October-November) when prices typically dip compared to peak season (June-September). Be flexible with your travel dates to find the most affordable options.

Mobile App Magic: Download the apps of these booking platforms. They sometimes offer exclusive mobile deals and last-minute discounts.

Loyalty Love: Sign up for the loyalty programs of your preferred booking platform. You might accumulate points redeemable for future stays or discounts.

Beyond the Big Boys: Unearthing Santorini Specialists

Small Luxury Hotels of the World (SLH): This platform curates a collection of boutique hotels and unique properties, perfect for those seeking an intimate and personalized experience. While these stays might come at a premium, SLH often offers special packages or seasonal deals.

Santorini-Specific Websites: Many local Santorini travel agencies and accommodation providers maintain their own websites. Explore these for hidden gems, last-minute deals, and unique finds, especially cave houses and traditional guesthouses you might not find on mainstream platforms.

Negotiation Ninja: Striking Deals Directly with Properties

Don't Be Shy to Haggle: Especially during shoulder seasons or the off-season (November-March), contacting hotels or guesthouses directly can be fruitful. You might be able to negotiate a better rate, particularly for longer stays. Explain your budget and inquire about any available discounts or promotions.

Resources for Deal Detectives: Unveiling Discount Codes

Retail Me Not & Travel + Leisure: These websites aggregate travel deals and discount codes for various booking platforms and travel providers. Search for Santorini-specific deals or coupons before finalizing your reservation.

Email Sign-Ups: Many hotels and travel agencies offer exclusive discounts and promotions to those subscribed to their email lists. Sign up for a few Santorini-based travel agencies or hotels you're interested in to receive alerts about special offers.

Remember: Price shouldn't be the sole factor. Read reviews, compare amenities, and ensure the location aligns with your priorities (caldera views, proximity to nightlife, etc.) to find the perfect balance between affordability and a memorable Santorini experience.

By combining the power of popular booking platforms, niche resources, and a dash of negotiation, you can transform yourself into a Santorini stay-scoring savant and find your ideal accommodation without breaking the bank. Now go forth and conquer that dream Santorini escape!

Chapter 8: Getting Around Santorini:

Navigating Santorini's Charm: A Guide to Internal Transportation

Santorini's dramatic landscapes and iconic villages beg to be explored. But with a car-free main caldera cliffside and various transportation options, choosing the best way to get around can be tricky. Fear not, intrepid adventurer! This guide explores the pros and cons of renting a car, using taxis, taking buses, and even venturing out on an ATV to help you conquer Santorini's internal transportation scene.

Renting a Car: Freedom and Flexibility

Pros: Offers the most freedom and flexibility to explore Santorini at your own pace. You can create your own itinerary, reach secluded beaches, and discover hidden gems off the beaten path.

Cons: Santorini's roads, especially in the caldera villages (Fira, Oia, etc.), can be narrow, winding, and crowded during peak season. Parking can also be a challenge, particularly in popular areas. International drivers will need an International Driving Permit (IDP).

Taxis: Convenience with a Price Tag

Pros: Taxis are readily available in most tourist areas, especially around bus terminals, Fira, and Oia. They offer a convenient way to get around, particularly for short distances or late-night travel when buses are less frequent.

Cons: Taxis can be expensive, especially for longer journeys. Fares are not always metered, so agree on a price upfront to avoid surprises. Availability can be limited, particularly during peak season.

Buses: Budget-Friendly Exploration

Pros: The most affordable way to travel around Santorini. The island boasts a well-organized bus network connecting major villages, beaches, and archaeological sites. Buses run frequently during peak season, making them a reliable option.

Cons: Buses can get crowded, especially during peak season. Travel times can be longer compared to taxis or cars due to designated stops. Bus schedules might be less frequent in the shoulder seasons and off-season.

Exploring by ATV: A Thrilling Adventure

Pros: ATVs offer a unique and adventurous way to explore Santorini's inland areas and lesser-known beaches. They are perfect for navigating off-road terrains and experiencing the island's volcanic landscapes.

Cons: ATVs can be dusty and noisy, especially during dry seasons. Safety is a concern, so ensure you're comfortable driving an ATV and wear a helmet. Some areas might restrict ATV access due to environmental concerns.

Choosing Your Ideal Ride:

Budget: Buses are the most economical option, followed by cars (considering gas prices and parking) and then taxis (most expensive).

Flexibility: Cars offer the most freedom, followed by ATVs (with limitations due to off-road access) and then taxis and buses (with designated routes and schedules).

Comfort: Taxis and air-conditioned cars provide the most comfort, followed by buses, and then ATVs (can be dusty and bumpy).

Number of Travelers: Cars and ATVs are ideal for small groups or couples, while buses are a good option for solo travelers or those on a tight budget.

Additional Tips:

Consider Combination Options: Mix and match your transportation options based on your needs. For example, use buses for longer journeys between villages and taxis for shorter distances or late-night travel.

Purchase a Bus Pass: If you plan on using buses frequently, consider purchasing a multi-day bus pass for cost savings.

Download Taxi Apps (if available): Some taxi companies in Santorini might have ride-hailing apps for easier booking and fare estimates.

By understanding the pros and cons of each transportation option, you can choose the one that best suits your travel style and budget. So, buckle up, adventurer, and get ready to explore the magic of Santorini!

Conquering Santorini's Internal Routes: A Guide to Costs, Schedules, and Navigation

Santorini's dramatic landscapes and iconic villages beckon exploration, but navigating the internal transportation network can be a puzzle. Fear not, intrepid traveler! This comprehensive guide delves into the costs, schedules, and navigation tips for renting cars, using taxis, taking buses, and even exploring via ATVs on Santorini.

Renting a Car: Freedom at Your Fingertips

Costs:
- Daily car rentals typically range from €40-€100 depending on car type, season, and rental agency.
- Factor in additional costs like gas (around €1.80 per liter) and parking fees (around €2-€5 per hour in popular areas).
- An International Driving Permit (IDP) is required for drivers with non-EU licenses.

Schedules: Car rental agencies are plentiful in Fira and Oia, with some operating at the airport. Opening hours vary, but many are open from 8:00 AM to 8:00 PM.

Navigation: Renting a car with GPS navigation is highly recommended, especially if you're unfamiliar with the island's narrow, winding roads. Many online car rental platforms allow you to add GPS as an extra during the booking process. Offline maps downloaded on your phone can be a backup option.

Taxis: Convenience with a Premium

Costs: Taxis operate on a meter system, but agree on the fare upfront, especially for longer journeys, to avoid surprises. Expect fares to start around €5 and increase based on distance and time.

Schedules: Taxis are readily available at designated taxi ranks in Fira, Oia, and other tourist areas. Hailing a taxi might be more challenging, especially during peak season. Consider calling a taxi company for pick-up if needed.

Navigation: Simply inform the taxi driver of your desired destination, and they'll handle the navigation.

Buses: Budget-Friendly Exploration

Costs: Bus tickets are very affordable, with single fares ranging from €1.80-€2.50 depending on the route. Consider purchasing a multi-day pass (€15-€20) for significant cost savings if you plan on using buses frequently.

Schedules: Buses operate from early morning until late evening during peak season (approximately from 6:00 AM to midnight). Frequency decreases in shoulder seasons and the off-season. Download the Santorini Public Bus app for live bus arrival information and route maps.

Navigation: Bus stops are well-marked throughout the island. Purchase tickets directly from the bus driver upon boarding. Validate your ticket on the machine onboard.

Exploring by ATV: An Adventurous Escapade

Costs: ATV rentals range from €40-€80 per day depending on the ATV type and rental agency. Gasoline costs are extra (around €1.80 per liter).

Schedules: ATV rental agencies are concentrated in Fira and Kamari. Opening hours vary, but many operate from 9:00 AM to 7:00 PM.

Navigation: While some rental agencies might provide basic maps, consider downloading offline navigation apps on your phone for better route guidance. Always prioritize safety and adhere to designated ATV routes to avoid restricted areas.

Choosing Your Ideal Ride:

Consider these factors when selecting your transportation mode:

Budget: Buses are the most economical, followed by cars (considering gas and parking), then taxis (most expensive).

Flexibility: Cars offer the most freedom, followed by ATVs (with limitations due to off-road access) and then taxis and buses (with designated routes and schedules).

Number of Travelers: Cars and ATVs are ideal for small groups, while buses are a good option for solo travelers or budget-conscious groups.

Additional Tips:

Plan Your Itinerary: Having a rough plan of the places you want to visit helps you choose the most efficient transportation mode.

Combine Options: Mix and match based on your needs. Use buses for longer journeys and taxis for shorter distances or late-night travel.

Learn Basic Greek Phrases: Knowing a few basic phrases like "ευχαριστώ" (efcharistó - thank you) and "πόσο κάνει;" (poso kánei - how much?) can be helpful when interacting with taxi drivers or bus ticket vendors.

With this knowledge in hand, you can navigate Santorini's transportation network like a seasoned explorer, unlocking the full potential of this captivating island paradise.

Part 3: Exploring Santorini

Chapter 9: Must-See Santorini Attractions:

Unveiling Santorini's Gems: A Must-See Sights Itinerary

Santorini's dramatic landscapes, charming villages, and volcanic wonders leave an indelible mark on any traveler. To help you navigate this captivating island, here's an outline of must-see sights, encompassing iconic locations, archaeological treasures, and volcanic adventures:

Caldera Cliffside Majesty: Oia and Fira

Unmissable Panoramas: Perched atop the caldera cliffs, Oia and Fira offer breathtaking views of the Aegean Sea. Wander the labyrinthine streets lined with whitewashed houses, azure-domed churches, and charming cafes.

Oia's Sunset Spectacle: Renowned for its legendary sunsets, Oia transforms into a sea of vibrant colors as the sun dips below the horizon. Witness this spectacle from the castle ruins or a restaurant terrace.

Akrotiri: A Buried Minoan City

Unearthing the Past: Embark on a journey back in time at the Akrotiri Archaeological Site. This Minoan settlement, buried by a volcanic eruption around 1600 BC, offers a glimpse into a bygone era. Explore preserved buildings, streets, and artifacts.

Volcanic Wonders: Nea Kameni & Palea Kameni

Active Volcanic Exploration: Take a boat tour to Nea Kameni, an active volcano in the caldera's center. Hike along the crater rim and witness volcanic vents releasing steam and sulfur fumes.

Palea Kameni's Geothermal Delights: Sail to Palea Kameni, known for its volcanic hot springs. Bathe in the mineral-rich waters, a rejuvenating experience amidst the volcanic landscape.

Beyond the Caldera Rim: Unveiling Santorini's Treasures

Prophet Elias Monastery: Hike or take a cable car to the island's highest point, where the Prophet Elias

Monastery stands. Be rewarded with panoramic vistas encompassing the entire island.

Santo Wines: A Taste of Santorini Immerse yourself in Santorini's unique wine culture by visiting a winery. Sample local wines produced from the volcanic soil, known for their distinct mineral character.

Colored Sand Beaches: A Volcanic Palette Santorini boasts a variety of colored sand beaches due to its volcanic origins. Explore the black sands of Perissa and Kamari beaches, the dramatic Red Beach near Akrotiri, or the pristine White Beach, accessible by boat.

Museum of Prehistoric Thera: Uncover Santorini's ancient past at the Museum of Prehistoric Thera. Explore archaeological exhibits showcasing artifacts from Akrotiri and other excavation sites, piecing together the island's rich history.

Planning Your Santorini Adventure:

Prioritize Based on Interests: Tailor your itinerary to your interests. Are you a sunset chaser, a history buff, or a volcanic explorer?

Allocate Time Wisely: Some destinations, like Akrotiri, require dedicated exploration time. Factor in travel time between locations.

Consider Tours: Guided tours can provide valuable insights and ensure efficient exploration, especially for archaeological sites.

With this guide in hand, start crafting your Santorini adventure. From iconic villages to volcanic wonders, this island paradise awaits your exploration!

Chapter 10: Off the Beaten Path:

Unveiling Santorini's Hidden Gems: Beyond the Caldera Crowds

Santorini's iconic villages and dramatic landscapes are mesmerizing, but venturing beyond the well-trodden tourist path unveils a treasure trove of hidden gems. Here's your guide to a more local Santorini experience:

Charming Villages: Escape the Crowds

Emporio: Nestled inland, Emporio offers a traditional charm often overshadowed by Fira and Oia. Wander the labyrinthine streets of the Venetian Castle, explore the charming main square, and discover local art galleries and shops.

Emporio village, Santorini

Megalochori: This village boasts a traditional atmosphere with cave houses built into the cliffs. Visit the charming Megalochori Clock Tower, sip local wine at a quaint winery, or enjoy a meal at a family-run taverna.

Megalochori village, Santorini

Pyrgos: Perched on a hilltop, Pyrgos offers stunning panoramic views and a laid-back atmosphere. Explore the ruins of the medieval castle, meander through narrow streets lined with whitewashed houses, and visit traditional tavernas for a taste of local cuisine.

Pyrgos village, Santorini

Unique Experiences: Unveiling Santorini's Soul

Cooking Classes: Immerse yourself in Greek culture by participating in a cooking class. Learn to prepare traditional Santorini dishes like fava beans, tomato fritters, and fresh seafood, using local ingredients.

Wine Tasting Beyond the Mainstream: Venture beyond the big wineries and discover smaller, family-run producers. Enjoy a personalized wine tasting experience paired with breathtaking caldera views or charming village settings.

Sailing Tours with a Twist: Instead of a crowded catamaran cruise, opt for a traditional sailboat tour with a local captain. Explore secluded coves inaccessible by land, snorkel in crystal-clear waters, and witness the sunset from a unique perspective.

Caldera Kayaking Adventure: Explore the caldera from a different angle with a kayaking tour. Paddle past volcanic islands, hidden coves, and dramatic cliffs, enjoying a unique perspective of Santorini's beauty.

Alternative Activities: Off the Beaten Path

Hike the Mesa Trail: Embark on a scenic hike along the Mesa Trail, an ancient footpath connecting Fira to Oia. Enjoy breathtaking views of the caldera, volcanic landscapes, and traditional villages along the way.

Mesa Trail, Santorini

Visit the Tomato Industrial Museum: Learn about Santorini's unique agricultural heritage at the Tomato Industrial Museum. Discover the history of tomato cultivation on the island and its significance to the local economy.

Tomato Industrial Museum, Santorini

Stargazing Extravaganza: Santorini, with minimal light pollution, boasts exceptional stargazing opportunities. Join a guided stargazing tour led by astronomy enthusiasts and be awestruck by the Milky Way and constellations.

Black Sand Yoga on Perissa Beach: Unwind and rejuvenate with a yoga session on Perissa Beach's volcanic black sand. The unique setting and calming sound of the waves create a truly unforgettable experience.

Tips for a Local Experience:

Learn a Few Greek Phrases: A few basic greetings and thank yous go a long way in establishing a connection with locals.

Engage with Local Shopkeepers: Venture beyond tourist shops and explore local markets and family-run stores. Interact with shopkeepers and discover unique handcrafted souvenirs.

Dine at Tavernas: Skip the tourist traps and savor authentic Greek cuisine at family-run tavernas. Enjoy fresh, locally-sourced ingredients and a welcoming atmosphere.

Embrace the Siesta: Respect the local custom of siesta, where many shops and businesses close during the afternoon heat. Use this time to relax at your accommodation or explore a shady village backstreet.

By following these recommendations, you can create a unique and authentic Santorini experience, venturing beyond the usual tourist hotspots and discovering the island's hidden gems and local charm.

Chapter 11: Hiking and Outdoor Activities:

Conquering Santorini's Trails: A Guide to Hiking Adventures

Santorini's dramatic landscapes are perfect for exploring on foot. Beyond the iconic villages, a network of hiking trails awaits, offering breathtaking views, volcanic vistas, and a chance to experience the island's natural beauty. Here's a breakdown of popular trails, difficulty levels, and safety tips for an unforgettable hiking adventure:

Moderate Hikes: Panoramic Delights

Fira to Oia (Distance: 7 km / 4.3 miles, Estimated Time: 2-3 hours): This classic route, Santorini's most popular hike, traverses the island's caldera rim, offering stunning panoramic views of the Aegean Sea, volcanic cliffs, and whitewashed villages. The path is well-maintained but can get crowded, especially during peak season.

Profitis Ilias to Perissa (Distance: 5 km / 3.1 miles, Estimated Time: 1.5-2 hours): This moderate hike starts near Santorini's highest point, Profitis Ilias Monastery. Descend through scenic valleys with dramatic volcanic landscapes and enjoy glimpses of the island's inland side. The trail splits halfway, with one path leading to Kamari and the other to Perissa, a beach village.

Easy Hikes: Leisurely Exploration

Megalochori to Pyrgos (Distance: 2 km / 1.2 miles, Estimated Time: 1 hour): This gentle stroll connects two charming villages. The path winds through vineyards, offering scenic countryside vistas and traditional cave houses. Enjoy a leisurely pace and stop at a winery for a local wine tasting experience.

Skaros Rock and Panagia Theoskepasti Trail (Distance: 2 km / 1.2 miles, Estimated Time: 45 minutes): This short hike near Imerovigli leads to Skaros Rock, a volcanic remnant with a ruined castle offering panoramic caldera views. Continue the trail to reach the quaint Panagia Theoskepasti church, known for its blue dome.

Challenging Hikes: For Experienced Hikers

Ancient Thera Trail (Distance: 4 km / 2.5 miles, Estimated Time: 1.5-2 hours): This challenging hike starts near Kamari Beach and leads to the archaeological site of Ancient Thera. The مسير (masir - path) is steep and rocky in sections, with loose gravel underfoot. Reward yourself with stunning views and a glimpse into Santorini's ancient past.

Safety Tips for Hiking in Santorini:

Plan Your Hike: Research the chosen trail, understand the difficulty level, and ensure it matches your fitness level.

Bring Appropriate Gear: Wear sturdy hiking shoes, comfortable clothing, and a hat. Sunscreen, sunglasses, and a refillable water bottle are essential.

Start Early: Especially during peak season, start your hike early to avoid the midday heat.

Be Sun Smart: Santorini has strong sunshine. Apply sunscreen regularly and re-apply after sweating.

Stay Hydrated: Drink plenty of water throughout your hike, especially in hot weather.

Respect the Environment: Stay on designated trails, avoid disturbing wildlife, and pack out all trash.

Mind Your Footing: The terrain can be uneven and rocky on some trails. Watch your step and wear shoes with good ankle support.

Inform Someone: Let someone know your planned route and estimated return time, especially if hiking alone.

Additional Tips:
- Download offline maps or consider a GPS device, especially for less-frequented trails.
- Carry a small first-aid kit in case of minor injuries.
- Pack a light snack for longer hikes.
- Be aware of potential for loose gravel or uneven surfaces on some trails.

With careful planning and an awareness of safety precautions, hiking in Santorini can be a rewarding and enriching experience. Lace up your boots, grab your backpack, and get ready to explore the island's hidden beauty and breathtaking scenery!

Unveiling Santorini's Outdoor Delights: Beyond Hiking Adventures

Santorini's dramatic landscapes and crystal-clear waters beckon for exploration beyond hiking trails. This guide delves into exhilarating water adventures, volcanic explorations, and unique boat tours, offering a plethora of outdoor activities to make your Santorini experience unforgettable.

Kayaking Adventures: A Paddler's Paradise

Explore the Caldera from a New Perspective: Embark on a kayaking tour around the caldera. Paddle past volcanic islands, hidden coves, and dramatic cliffs, enjoying a unique vantage point of Santorini's beauty. Half-day and full-day tours with experienced guides are available, catering to various skill levels.

Snorkeling Delights: Combine kayaking with snorkeling adventures. Many tours include stops at secluded bays with vibrant marine life, allowing you to explore the underwater world.

Sunset Kayaking: Witness the awe-inspiring Santorini sunset from a kayak. Glide across the calm waters as the sky erupts in a kaleidoscope of colors, creating a truly magical experience.

Volcanic Island Exploration: Nea Kameni & Palea Kameni

Nea Kameni's Active Volcanic Landscape: Take a volcanic exploration tour to Nea Kameni, an active volcano in the caldera's center. Hike along the crater rim, witness volcanic vents spewing steam and sulfur fumes, and marvel at the lunar-like landscape. Tours typically include a boat ride and may even offer the opportunity to swim in nearby hot springs.

Palea Kameni's Geothermal Delights: Sail to Palea Kameni, known for its volcanic hot springs. Bathe in the mineral-rich waters, a rejuvenating experience amidst the volcanic landscape. Combine a visit to Palea Kameni with a trip to Nea Kameni for a comprehensive volcanic exploration.

Unforgettable Boat Tours: Discover Santorini's Secrets

Catamaran Cruises with a Twist: Opt for a smaller, semi-private catamaran cruise instead of a crowded mass tour. Enjoy a more personalized experience with a relaxed atmosphere, allowing for swimming stops, delicious meals, and breathtaking caldera views.

Sunset Sails: Set sail on a romantic sunset cruise and witness the fiery spectacle as the sun dips below the horizon, painting the sky with vibrant hues. Enjoy delicious food, drinks, and the gentle Aegean breeze as you soak in the magical atmosphere.

Fishing Tours: Experience Santorini from a local's perspective with a fishing tour. Learn traditional fishing techniques, enjoy the thrill of catching your own dinner, and savor fresh seafood onboard with breathtaking views.

Additional Outdoor Activities:

Stand-Up Paddleboarding: Glide across the calm Aegean waters on a stand-up paddleboard. Explore hidden coves and enjoy a unique way to experience Santorini's coastline.

Windsurfing and Kitesurfing: For adrenaline seekers, windsurfing and kitesurfing lessons and rentals are available, especially in southern Santorini with its stronger winds.

Scuba Diving: Explore the underwater world around Santorini with a scuba diving excursion. Discover vibrant marine life, volcanic rock formations, and shipwrecks for a truly unique adventure (proper certification required).

Choosing Your Perfect Outdoor Adventure:

Consider Your Interests: Are you a thrill-seeker craving adventure, or do you prefer a relaxing kayaking excursion? Choose activities that align with your preferences.

Travel with Children: Opt for family-friendly activities like kayaking tours with calm water sections or boat cruises with amenities for children.

Weather Conditions: Certain activities like windsurfing are more suitable during windier seasons.

Santorini's outdoor playground offers something for everyone. So lace up your hiking boots, grab your swimsuit, or hop on a boat, and get ready to experience the magic of this extraordinary island!

Part 4: Living the Santorini Life

Chapter 12: Food and Drink:

A Culinary Journey Through Santorini: Unveiling Local Flavors

Santorini's culinary scene is as captivating as its landscapes. Fresh, local ingredients infused with volcanic soil characteristics create unique flavors. Beyond the stunning views, embark on a delicious adventure with Santorini's must-try dishes, exceptional wines, and the best spots to savor authentic flavors.

Tantalizing Santorini Specialties:

Fava Me Koukia: This creamy fava bean dip, a staple in Santorini households, is a delightful appetizer or light meal. Enjoy it drizzled with local olive oil and crusty bread.

111

Fava Me Koukia Santorini

Domatokeftedes: These fried tomato fritters, bursting with fresh Santorini tomatoes, herbs, and spices, are a vegetarian delight. Savor them with a dollop of creamy tzatziki sauce.

Domatokeftedes Santorini

Chlorotyri: This brined cheese, unique to Santorini, boasts a tangy flavor and creamy texture. Enjoy it sliced in a salad, crumbled over pasta dishes, or simply savor it on its own with a drizzle of olive oil and local honey.

Chlorotyri Santorini

Grilled Octopus: Freshly caught octopus, simply grilled to perfection, is a must-try for seafood lovers. The smoky flavor complements the natural sweetness of the octopus.

Santorini Salad: This refreshing salad features capers, a Santorini specialty, alongside cherry tomatoes, cucumbers, onions, and local cheese. Dressed with a light olive oil and vinegar vinaigrette, it's a perfect accompaniment to any meal.

Fresh Seafood Delights:

Santorinian Lobster: Indulge in the local spiny lobster, a star of Santorini's seafood scene. Prepared simply grilled, baked, or in a flavorful stew, the lobster's delicate sweetness shines through.

Swordfish Souvlaki: Marinated chunks of swordfish threaded onto skewers and grilled to perfection are a quintessential Santorini dish. Enjoy it with a side of Santorini fava or roasted vegetables.

Unique Santorini Wines:

Assyrtiko Grape: The volcanic soil and sunny climate create a unique character for Santorini's wines. Assyrtiko, the dominant grape variety, produces crisp white wines with a mineral edge.

Vinsanto: This dessert wine, made from sun-dried Assyrtiko grapes, boasts a rich, amber color and complex flavor profile. Enjoy it as an after-dinner treat or paired with local cheese.

Experiencing Authentic Santorini Dining:

Family-Run Tavernas: Venture beyond tourist traps and seek out family-run tavernas in charming villages. These establishments offer a warm atmosphere, friendly service, and a chance to savor traditional home-cooked meals.

Vineyard Tastings: Embark on a journey through Santorini's unique wines by visiting a local winery. Sample various Assyrtiko wines and learn about the winemaking process amidst the beautiful caldera or vineyard settings.

Cooking Classes: Immerse yourself in Greek culture by participating in a cooking class. Learn to prepare traditional Santorini dishes from scratch, using fresh, local ingredients, under the guidance of experienced chefs.

Beyond the Plate: Setting the Scene

Cliffside Dining with a View: For a truly unforgettable experience, choose a restaurant perched on the caldera cliffs. Savor delicious food while marveling at the breathtaking panoramic views of the Aegean Sea and the volcanic landscape.

Village Charm: Dine at a taverna in a traditional village like Oia, Emporio, or Megalochori. Enjoy the local atmosphere, savor authentic flavors, and soak in the charm of Santorini's villages.

Embrace the Local Dining Culture:

Linger Over Your Meal: Santorini dining is a leisurely affair. Slow down, savor the flavors, and enjoy the company.

Seasonal Specialties: Ask about the daily specials and opt for dishes featuring fresh, seasonal ingredients.

Embrace Meze: Experience the Greek tradition of meze, a selection of small plates meant for sharing. Sample a variety of dishes and enjoy the social aspect of dining.

With its delectable cuisine, fresh seafood, and unique wines, Santorini offers a culinary adventure unlike any other. So venture beyond the usual tourist fare, explore local tavernas, and embark on a delicious journey that tantalizes your taste buds and complements your Santorini experience.

Chapter 13: Shopping in Santorini:

Santorini Staples: Souvenirs to Spark Memories

Santorini Miniatures: Replicate Santorini's iconic scenery in miniature form. Find charming miniature houses, churches, and windmills, all painted in the traditional white and blue hues. These are a delightful way to remember the island's beauty.

Santorini miniature houses souvenirs

Santorini Donkey Figurines: Donkeys have been a traditional mode of transportation on Santorini for centuries. Commemorate these hardworking animals with a ceramic or wooden donkey figurine, a popular tourist souvenir.

Evil Eye Charms: Apotropaic evil eye charms are a common sight throughout Greece. Find these talismans in various shapes, sizes, and colors, believed to ward off misfortune. They make a unique and cultural souvenir.

Evil Eye Santorini souvenir

Local Crafts and Handmade Treasures:

Woven Baskets and Textiles: Explore the vibrant world of Santorini's woven goods. Find beautiful baskets, handwoven with local straw, perfect for storing trinkets or as decorative items for your home. Colorful textiles, handwoven on traditional looms, are another exquisite option.

Santorini Sandals: Step into comfort and style with a pair of handmade Santorini sandals. Locally crafted from genuine leather, these sandals come in various designs and colors, offering a touch of Santorini chic to any outfit.

Santorini Sandals Santorini souvenir

Ceramic Artwork: Santorini boasts a rich tradition of ceramic art. Find beautiful plates, bowls, vases, and decorative items adorned with intricate designs and traditional motifs. These pieces add a touch of Santorini charm to your home.

Santorini Ceramic Artwork souvenir

Specialty Santorini Products: A Taste of the Island

Santorini Wine: Take home a bottle (or two) of Santorini's unique wine as a souvenir. Assyrtiko, the island's signature grape variety, produces crisp white wines with a mineral edge. Opt for a bottle from a local winery you visit for an extra special memento.

Santorini Wine Santorini souvenir

Santorini Honey: Santorini's volcanic soil imparts a unique flavor to its honey. Purchase a jar of this local delicacy, known for its rich taste and golden color. Enjoy it on its own, drizzle it over cheese or yogurt, or use it in baking.

Santorini Honey Santorini souvenir

Capers: Santorini is renowned for its capers, the flower buds of the caper bush. These briny and piquant flavor bombs are a versatile ingredient used in Greek cuisine. Bring back a jar to add a unique touch to your dishes back home.

Santorini Capers Santorini souvenir

Tips for Savvy Shopping:

Explore Local Markets: Venture beyond tourist shops and explore local markets for a more authentic shopping experience. Interact with local vendors, discover unique handmade crafts, and find better deals.

Haggling is Expected: In some shops, particularly at flea markets, friendly haggling is expected. Do so politely and respectfully to potentially score a good bargain.

Look for Quality Craftsmanship: When buying handmade items, inspect the quality of materials and craftsmanship. This ensures you get a beautiful and long-lasting piece.

Support Local Artisans: By purchasing from local artisans and shops, you directly contribute to Santorini's economy and preserve its traditional crafts.

Santorini's shopping scene offers something for everyone. So delve into the charming shops, explore local markets, and bring back a piece of Santorini's magic to cherish for years to come!

Chapter 14: Nightlife and Entertainment:

Unveiling Santorini's Nightlife: From Cocktail Bars to Caldera Beats

Santorini's vibrant nightlife caters to diverse preferences. Whether you crave sunset cocktails with breathtaking views, energetic dance floors, or a relaxed atmosphere with live music, the island offers something for every night owl. Here's a glimpse into Santorini's after-dark scene:

Fira's Buzzing Heart: Bars and Clubs Galore

Koo Club: Renowned as Fira's top club, Koo offers an indoor-outdoor dance experience. With crystal chandeliers, glittering disco balls, and world-class DJs spinning the latest tunes, prepare for a night of revelry.

Koo Club Santorini

Enigma Club: This lively club boasts a dance floor and a spacious terrace, perfect for enjoying the caldera views under the starlit sky. Get ready for energetic music and a fun-filled atmosphere.

Enigma Club Santorini

Town Club: Open 24/7, Town Club is a popular spot for late-night revelers. Dance the night away to a mix of music genres, or simply relax with a drink and enjoy the lively ambiance.

PK Cocktail Bar: This sophisticated bar is a haven for cocktail connoisseurs. Expert mixologists craft innovative and classic cocktails using premium ingredients, perfect for a sophisticated evening.

Franco's Bar: For a more relaxed vibe, head to Franco's Bar. Enjoy stunning sunset views from the terrace, sip on handcrafted cocktails, and soak in the vibrant atmosphere.

Beyond Fira's Buzz: Alternative Nightlife Experiences

Oia's Sunset Strolls and Cocktail Bars: While not as club-centric as Fira, Oia offers a charming nightlife scene. Stroll through the picturesque village at sunset, stopping at a bar with a caldera view for a romantic cocktail experience.

Wine Bars with a View: Santorini's wineries often extend their hours into the evening. Enjoy a unique experience by sipping on local wines at a winery bar, often accompanied by breathtaking caldera vistas and live music.

Live Music Tavernas: Immerse yourself in Greek culture at a taverna with live music. Savor delicious food, enjoy traditional music performances, and experience the warmth of Greek hospitality.

Tips for an Enjoyable Night Out:

Dress Code: While there's no strict dress code, most bars and clubs have a smart casual vibe. For upscale establishments, opt for slightly dressier attire.

Reservations Recommended: Popular bars and clubs, especially during peak season, may require reservations. Plan ahead to avoid disappointment.

Transportation: Public transportation can be limited at night. Consider taxis or pre-arrange transportation back to your accommodation.

Safety First:

Drink Responsibly: Pace yourself and enjoy drinks responsibly throughout the night.

Be Mindful of Your Belongings: Keep an eye on your belongings, especially in crowded bars and clubs.

Santorini's nightlife scene offers a vibrant mix of energetic dance floors, sophisticated cocktail bars, and relaxed tavernas. So, choose your vibe, explore the options, and prepare to paint the town red (or Santorini's signature blue!) Just remember to drink responsibly, prioritize safety, and embrace the island's unique after-dark energy.

Tailoring Santorini's Nightlife to Your Preferences and Age Group

Santorini's nightlife caters to a variety of preferences and age groups. Whether you're a young partygoer, a couple seeking romance, or a group of friends wanting a relaxed evening, here's a guide to finding the perfect spot:

For the Young and Energetic:

Fira's Bustling Clubs: Embrace the vibrant energy of Fira's clubs like Koo or Enigma. Dance the night away to the latest beats under dazzling lights and enjoy the electric atmosphere. (Age group: 21-35)

Town Club: This 24/7 club caters to late-night revelers. Enjoy a mix of music genres, a lively ambiance, and the option to dance or simply relax with a drink. (Age group: 21-35)

For the Romantics:

Oia's Sunset Cocktail Bars: Savor breathtaking sunset views from a charming bar in Oia. Sip on handcrafted cocktails, enjoy the romantic atmosphere, and create unforgettable memories with your loved one. (All Age Groups)

Wine Bars with a Caldera View: Combine romance with local flavors. Visit a winery bar with caldera views, indulge in delicious Santorini wines, and soak in the magical atmosphere under the starlit sky. (All Age Groups)

For the Relaxed Crowd:

Live Music Tavernas: Immerse yourselves in Greek culture at a taverna with live music. Enjoy traditional food, delightful music performances, and the warmth of Greek hospitality. (All Age Groups)

Fira's Cocktail Bars (Select Venues): Fira isn't just about clubs. Explore sophisticated cocktail bars like PK Cocktail Bar for a refined experience with expertly crafted drinks in a relaxed setting. (Age Group: 25 and up)

For Mature Travelers:

Wine Tastings with Evening Events: Several wineries host special evening events with wine tastings, live music, and delicious food pairings. Enjoy a sophisticated and relaxing evening surrounded by beautiful scenery. (All Age Groups, though may be more suitable for those who appreciate wine and a calmer atmosphere)

Sunset Sails with Dinner: Embark on a romantic sunset sail and enjoy a delicious dinner on board. Witness the breathtaking Santorini sunset from a unique perspective, creating a truly memorable experience. (All Age Groups)

Additional Considerations:

Dress Code: While Santorini leans casual, some upscale bars and clubs may suggest a smart casual dress code.

Live Music Schedules: Research live music tavernas and their performance schedules to ensure you catch your favorite tunes.

Transportation: Public transport after dark can be limited. Consider taxis or pre-arranging transportation back to your accommodation.

Remember:

Drink Responsibly: No matter your age or preference, always prioritize responsible drinking habits.

Safety First: Keep an eye on your belongings and be mindful of your surroundings, especially in crowded areas.

Embrace the Culture: Santorini's nightlife offers a unique experience. Be open to trying new things and soak in the island's vibrant atmosphere.

With a little planning and this guide in hand, you can find the perfect nightlife experience in Santorini, no matter your age or preference. So, let loose, have fun, and create lasting memories under the Santorini sky!

Part 5: Essential Information

Chapter 15: Staying Connected:

Staying Connected in Santorini: A Guide to WiFi, SIM Cards & Roaming

Staying connected in Santorini is important for sharing photos, navigating the island, and keeping in touch with loved ones back home. Here's a breakdown of your options for WiFi access, local SIM cards, and international roaming:

WiFi Availability:

Most Accommodations Offer WiFi: The vast majority of hotels, apartments, and villas in Santorini offer WiFi to their guests, typically included in the accommodation rate. However, connection speeds and reliability can vary.

Public WiFi Hotspots: Limited free WiFi hotspots are scattered around Santorini, mainly in Fira, Oia, and other popular tourist spots. The connection speed and reliability might be lower compared to private networks.

Restaurants and Cafes: Many restaurants and cafes offer WiFi access for their customers. This can be a convenient option if you need to connect while grabbing a coffee or enjoying a meal.

Purchasing a Local SIM Card:

Mobile Network Providers: Santorini has two major mobile network providers: Cosmote and Vodafone. You can purchase prepaid SIM cards with data packages at their physical stores located in Fira and other main villages.

Benefits: A local SIM card offers peace of mind with reliable data access throughout your stay. It's also generally cheaper than relying solely on international roaming charges.

Considerations: Ensure your phone is unlocked to use a SIM card from a different provider. Compare data package options and choose one that suits your needs.

International Roaming:

Contact Your Mobile Provider: Before your trip, contact your mobile network provider to inquire about international roaming charges in Greece. These charges can be expensive, so it's important to be aware of the costs before using your phone's data or making calls.

Roaming Packages: Some mobile providers offer special roaming packages that can be more cost-effective than standard charges. Explore these options to see if they make sense for your trip.

Here's a quick comparison to help you decide:

Option	Pros	Cons
Accommo dation WiFi	Often included, convenient	Speed and reliability can vary
Public WiFi	Free	Limited availability, slower speeds
Local SIM Card	Reliable data access, potentially cheaper than roaming	Requires unlocked phone, need to purchase a SIM card

Internatio nal Roaming	No additional setup needed	Potentially expensive charges, data usage can quickly add up

Additional Tips:

Download Offline Maps and Resources: Before your trip, download offline maps and essential travel resources on your phone in case you encounter limited WiFi access.

Consider a Portable WiFi Hotspot: If you need reliable internet access throughout your stay for multiple devices, consider renting a portable WiFi hotspot. These devices provide a personal WiFi network wherever you go in Santorini.

Be Mindful of Data Usage: If you're using a local SIM card with a data package, be mindful of your data usage to avoid exceeding your limit and incurring additional charges.

By considering your needs and budget, you can choose the most suitable option for staying connected in Santorini. Enjoy your trip!

Chapter 16: Culture and Customs:

Unveiling Greek Culture and Customs: A Handy Guide

Greek culture, steeped in history, mythology, and tradition, offers a warm welcome to visitors. Here's a quick overview of essential customs and etiquette to navigate your trip to Santorini:

Dress Code for Religious Sites:
- Respectful Attire: When visiting churches and monasteries, both men and women should dress modestly. This means covering shoulders and knees. Avoid sleeveless shirts, short shorts, or revealing clothing.
- Scarves and Wraps: If your outfit doesn't meet the criteria, bring a scarf or light wrap to cover up before entering religious sites. Some churches may also offer visitors head coverings for women.

Tipping Etiquette:
- Tipping is Not Mandatory: Unlike some countries, tipping in Greece is not obligatory. However, it's a nice way to show appreciation for good service.
- Small Gestures: If you've received excellent service at a restaurant, bar, or with taxi drivers, a small tip of 5-10% of the bill is customary. You can simply round up the bill or leave a few euros on the table.
- No Need to Tip for Everything: Tipping isn't expected at cafes, for small purchases, or for services already included in the bill.

Common Greetings:
- Γεια σας (Yá sas): This is the most common greeting, meaning "Hello" and can be used in most situations.
- Καλημέρα (Kaliméra): Used specifically for "Good morning."
- Καλησπέρα (Kalaspéra): Used specifically for "Good evening."
- Γεια σας! Πώς τα πάτε; (Yá sas! Pós ta páte?): This is a more formal greeting that translates to "Hello! How are you?"

Additional Tips:

Learn a Few Basic Greek Phrases: Learning a few basic phrases like "Thank you" (Ευχαριστώ - Efkharistó) and "Please" (Παρακαλώ - Parakalo) goes a long way in showing respect for the local culture.

Respect Personal Space: Greeks tend to stand a bit closer than people from some cultures during conversations. Be mindful of personal space but don't feel offended if someone seems closer than you're used to.

Relax and Enjoy the Vibe: Greeks are known for their relaxed and friendly nature. Embrace the slower pace of life and enjoy the warm hospitality.

By understanding these basic cultural aspects, you can ensure a smooth and respectful experience while navigating Santorini and beyond in Greece. So, immerse yourself in the rich tapestry of Greek culture, and create lasting memories on your travels!

Chapter 17: Safety and Security:

Safety First: Essential Tips for a Secure Santorini Adventure

Santorini is a generally safe island for tourists, but as with any travel destination, a little preparation and awareness go a long way. Here's a breakdown of safety tips to ensure a secure and enjoyable Santorini experience:

General Precautions:

Be Mindful of Your Belongings: Petty theft can occur, especially in crowded areas. Keep an eye on your purse, wallet, and phone, particularly on public transportation and at tourist attractions.

Carry Important Documents Securely: Make copies of your passport and important documents. Leave the originals in a safe at your accommodation and carry only the copies with you.

Beware of Pickpockets: In crowded places, be particularly vigilant against pickpockets. Avoid carrying large sums of cash and keep valuables close to your body. Consider a money belt for added security.

Alert Someone of Your Plans: Let your family or friends back home know your itinerary and accommodation details, especially if you're planning solo travel.

Respecting the Environment:

Stay on Designated Trails: While exploring Santorini's volcanic landscapes and hiking trails, stick to designated paths to avoid damaging the fragile ecosystem.

Minimize Waste: Carry a reusable water bottle and avoid single-use plastics. Dispose of trash responsibly in designated bins.

Respect Local Customs: Dress modestly when visiting churches and monasteries. Be mindful of noise levels in public areas, especially near residential areas.

Staying Safe While Exploring:

Sun Safety: Santorini's sun is strong. Apply sunscreen generously and reapply frequently, especially after swimming. Wear a hat and sunglasses for additional protection.

Hydration is Key: Santorini's warm climate can lead to dehydration quickly. Carry a refillable water bottle and sip on water regularly throughout the day.

Beware of Slippery Surfaces: The volcanic terrain can be uneven with loose gravel or volcanic rock. Wear sturdy shoes with good grip, especially while hiking or exploring uneven paths.

Swim Safely: Obey all posted signs and warnings at beaches. Avoid swimming in areas with strong currents or when lifeguards are not on duty.

ATV Safety: ATV rentals are popular, but exercise caution. Only rent from reputable companies, wear a helmet, and ride defensively, especially on narrow roads.

Additional Tips:

Learn Basic First Aid: Equip yourself with a small first-aid kit containing essential supplies for minor injuries like cuts or scrapes.

Purchase Travel Insurance: Consider travel insurance to cover any unexpected medical emergencies or trip cancellations.

Emergency Numbers: Familiarize yourself with local emergency numbers for police (100), ambulance (166), and fire (199) in case of an emergency.

By following these safety tips and exercising common sense, you can minimize risks and ensure a worry-free Santorini adventure. Now you can focus on exploring the island's beauty, indulging in delicious food, and creating unforgettable memories!

Chapter 18: Useful Phrases in Greek:

Handy Greek Phrases for Santorini Travelers:

- Γεια σας (Yá sas): Hello (most common greeting)
- Καλημέρα (Kaliméra): Good morning
- Καλησπέρα (Kalaspéra): Good evening
- Αντίο (Αντίο σας) (Andío) (Andío sas): Goodbye (informal/formal)
- Παρακαλώ (Parakalo): Please
- Ευχαριστώ (Efkharistó): Thank you
- Ναι (Ne): Yes
- Όχι (Óchi): No
- Συγγνώμη (Signómi): Excuse me
- Χαίρομαι (Χαίρεσαι) (Chérome) (Chérese): Nice to meet you (formal/informal)
- Σας ευχαριστώ πολύ (Sas efkharistó polý): Thank you very much
- Δεν καταλαβαίνω (Den katalavéno): I don't understand
- Μιλάτε Αγγλικά; (Miláte Angliká?): Do you speak English?

- Πόσο κάνει; (Póso kání?): How much is this?
- Νερό (Neró): Water
- Καφές (Kafés): Coffee
- Μπίρα (Μπíra): Beer
- Κρασί (Krasí): Wine
- Ευχαριστώ, δεν καπνίζω (Efkharistó, den kapnízo): Thank you, I don't smoke
- Νόμισμα (Nómisma): Coin
- Χαρτονόμισμα (Chartonómisma): Bill
- Τουαλέτα (Toualéta): Toilet

Bonus Chapter:

Santorini Itineraries Tailored for Different Travel Styles

Santorini, with its dramatic cliffs, caldera views, charming villages, and delicious cuisine, caters to a variety of travel styles and durations. Here are some sample itineraries for short getaways, week-long explorations, and extended stays, designed to give you a taste of the island's magic:

Short Weekend Getaway (2-3 Days):

Day 1: Arrive in Santorini, check into your hotel in Fira or Oia, and explore the charming village streets. Indulge in a delicious seafood lunch overlooking the caldera. In the afternoon, visit the Prehistoric Museum of Thera to delve into Santorini's ancient history.

Prehistoric Museum of Thera Santorini

Day 2: Embark on a morning catamaran cruise around the caldera. Swim in the volcanic waters near Palea

Kameni and admire the volcanic rock formations. In the afternoon, explore the village of Megalochori, known for its traditional cave houses and wineries. Enjoy a wine tasting experience and savor the island's unique wines.

Catamaran cruise Santorini caldera

Day 3: Spend the morning relaxing on a black sand beach like Kamari or Perissa. Enjoy swimming, sunbathing, and water sports activities (optional). In the afternoon, head to Oia to witness the breathtaking sunset over the caldera, a quintessential Santorini experience. Enjoy a farewell dinner at a restaurant with caldera views.

Perissa Santorini beach

One-Week Exploration (5-7 Days):

Days 1-2: Follow the itinerary above for the short weekend getaway, exploring Fira, Oia, the caldera via a catamaran cruise, and the village of Megalochori.

Day 3: Hike from Fira to Oia, a scenic trail along the caldera cliffs offering stunning views. Allow plenty of time for photos and enjoy the dramatic volcanic landscape. In the afternoon, visit the Akrotiri Archaeological Site, an incredibly preserved Minoan settlement buried by volcanic ash.

Akrotiri Archaeological Site Santorini

Day 4: Take a day trip to nearby Nea Kameni, a volcanic island accessible by boat. Hike to the crater and witness the active volcanic vents releasing steam and sulfur fumes. In the afternoon, relax on a beach or explore the village of Emporio, known for its narrow alleys and traditional Cycladic architecture.

Emporio Santorini village

Day 5: Dedicate this day to exploring Santorini's culinary scene. Take a cooking class to learn how to prepare traditional Greek dishes using local ingredients. In the afternoon, visit a winery in Pyrgos village and indulge in a wine tasting experience with panoramic views.

Pyrgos Santorini village

Day 6: Rent an ATV and explore the island's hidden gems at your own pace. Visit the ancient ruins of Ancient Thera, offering breathtaking views and historical significance. In the afternoon, relax on a beach or visit the village of Vothonas, known for its donkey rides and panoramic vistas.

Vothonas Santorini village

Day 7: Spend a relaxing morning at your hotel or explore any final spots you missed. Do some souvenir shopping at local shops and enjoy a farewell lunch before departing Santorini.

Extended Stay (One Week or More):

With more time, delve deeper into Santorini's culture, history, and off-the-beaten-path experiences. Here are some additional options to consider:

Hiking and Outdoor Activities: Explore Santorini's diverse hiking trails, ranging from the challenging trek to the top of Mount Profitis Ilias to scenic coastal paths. Go kayaking or stand-up paddleboarding for a unique perspective of the caldera.

Hike Mount Profitis Ilias Santorini

Cultural Immersion: Take a Greek language class, participate in a traditional dance workshop, or learn about local crafts like pottery making or basket weaving.

Pottery making class Santorini

Volunteer Opportunities: Contribute to a local cause by volunteering at an animal shelter, participating in a beach clean-up, or assisting with archaeological projects.